Jellybean

A Baby's Journey to God

by Theoni and Bastian Bell
Illustrated by Bernadette Gockowski

Text copyright © 2024 by Theoni and Bastian Bell.
All rights reserved.
Artwork copyright © 2024 by Bernadette Gockowski.
All rights reserved.
No part of this book may be reproduced by any means
without the written permission of the publisher.

Excerpts from the English translation of *The Roman Missal* © 2010,
International Commission on English in the Liturgy Corporation.
All rights reserved. Used with permission.
Printed in the United States of America
ISBN: 978-1-959418-16-0

Published by Holy Heroes, LLC.
www.HolyHeroes.com

Helping You Bring the Joy of the Faith to Your Family

Presented to

_____

from

_____

In memory of

_____

In the beginning, Baby was
no bigger than a grain of sand.
She floated like a speck of pollen
until she found a place to land.

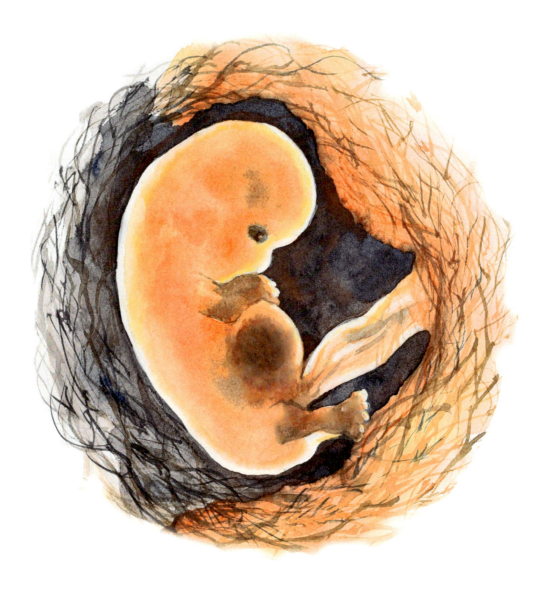

It was soft in Mother's belly
and snug as a mouse's hollow,
A place to be fed and cared for,
like the nest of a baby swallow.

And there she rested until one day
she heard the world beyond.
That day, she learned that people lived
outside her little pond.

Mother's voice was loudest.
She liked to hear it night and day.
She'd wake her mom with toe pokes
in hopes that they could play.

"Hi, there, tiny Jellybean,"
she heard her mother say.
To hear that voice again,
Baby danced a small ballet.

She liked the others too—
There was chirpy, chatty, and deep.
And when they called her "Jellybean,"
like John the Baptist, she'd leap.

She heard Sister's constant chitchat
with all her plastic playmates,
and Dad performing ad lib
like he did on all their playdates.

Brother's mouth was full of sound.
His play was full of *BOOM!*
Swishing swords and rumbling cars—
she loved when he went "VROOM!"

When fast asleep, a tuneful voice
roused Baby in the day.
A gentle pressing from above
made her world of water sway.

When Baby finally flipped
and let out a big round yawn,
The voice sang, "Morning, sleepyhead,"
as sweet as birds at dawn.

Baby could not wait to come out;
she wanted to meet them all!
She was no longer a jellybean—
her home had grown too small.

She was squished with her head high
and squished with her head low;
no matter how she turned,
there was little room to grow!

Listen! A new voice now,
close as her own beating heart,
as tender and joyful as Mother's,
yet not muffled and worlds apart.

It said, "My Son sent me to bring you
to meet your Heavenly Father
in His house of happy children.
So, come! Rise up, dear daughter!"

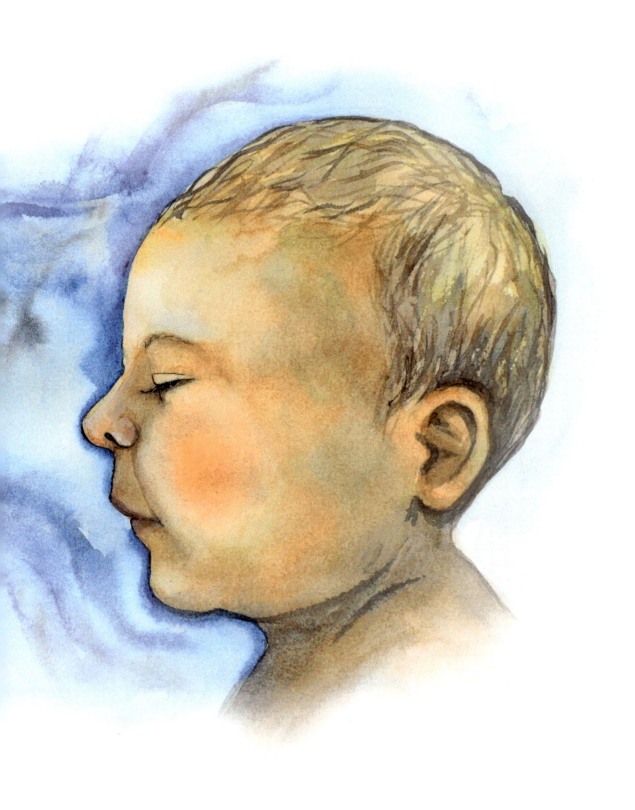

Jellybean felt a summer wind
breathe warm upon her skin,
and the flutter of butterfly wings
stirring her spirit deep within.

This was the voice to guide her out,
this star above the sea.
And even as she left her home,
she felt security.

Our Lady swooped Baby up in her arms.
They gazed at each other in rapture,
but Baby could hear that crying
had replaced her family's laughter.

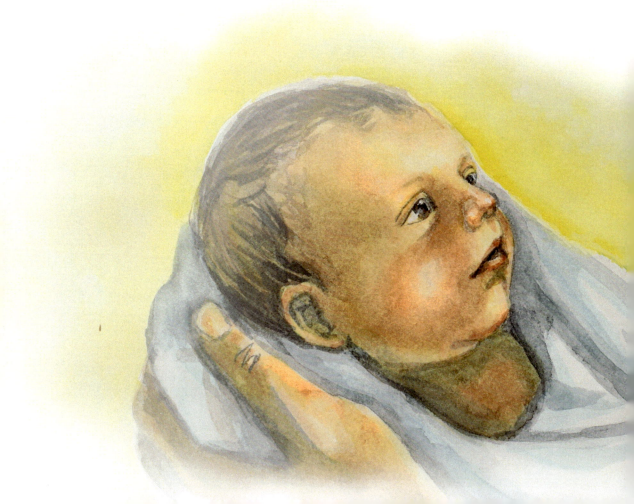

What about them? Are they coming too?
Our Lady said, "They must stay,
and they're going to need your help
to join you in Heaven one day."

Our Lady spoke and pressed her close,
their hearts beating together,
"My Son will calm their rocking boat
in the harshest of all weather."

"My Son will send His angels
to guide them through this loss.
The prayers and love of friends
will help them bear their cross.

If they bring their tears to Him
He will grant them what they need.
His grace will make a stronger faith
spring from the saddest seed."

Baby had joined a great sea of souls
singing delighted before a throne.
A hand reached out. A small voice said,
"Your family can't get here all on their own."

"I know you wish they had come,
but listen—you can hear them still.
You can ask the Lord face-to-face
to give them His grace, and He will."

In a FLASH, Baby was free.
One beat! And Baby could SEE.
Standing before the throne
her heart buzzed like a bumblebee.

Here there is no feeling squished.
There is no need to grow.
Safe from the sorrows on Earth,
Love is all she'll ever know.

Now Baby *can* hear their voices again—
the chatty, the chirpy, the deep.
One is feeling sad inside;
another is too scared to sleep.

"Are you there, Baby?" cries Mother,
sounding confused and alone.
I'm here. I'm here. Do not lose hope,
Baby utters in unspoken tones.

Whether sitting in traffic or in a church pew,

Know that my prayers will be always for you.

I will plead with Our Lord to grant you the grace

to join me one day in His loving embrace.

O God, searcher of hearts and most loving consoler,

Who know the faith of these parents,

grant that, as they mourn their child,

now departed from this life,

they may be assured

that he (she) has been entrusted

to Your Divine Compassion.

Through our Lord Jesus Christ, Your Son,

Who lives and reigns with You

in the unity of the Holy Spirit,

one God, for ever and ever.

— *Collect for the Funeral of a Child Who Died before Baptism*

Helping You Bring the Joy of the Faith to Your Family

To find more resources to help your family in this time, go to *holyheroes.com/loss*

Bastian and Theoni Bell live in Houston with their three children. They have four children in heaven and wrote Jellybean after the stillbirth of their daughter Sloane. Theoni is the author of several Catholic books for children and teens. You can find them at www.theonibell.com

Bernadette Gockowski is a Catholic artist and illustrator living in Wisconsin with her husband and five children. After losing three of her unborn babies, she finds joy in helping other mothers grieving the loss of an unborn baby in various ways. Illustrating Jellybean was a unique combination of these two passions, and she personally dedicated her work to all the parents she has met who grieve the loss of an unborn child.

WHAT SPREADING
THE GOSPEL MEANS
TO U.S. CHRISTIANS
IN THE 21ST CENTURY

TRANSLATING THE GREAT COMMISSION

A BARNA REPORT PRODUCED IN
PARTNERSHIP WITH SEED COMPANY

Copyright ©2018 by Barna Group. All rights reserved.

ISBN: 978-1-945269-16-5

All information contained in this document is copyrighted by Barna Group and shall remain the property of Barna Group. U.S. and international copyright laws protect the contents of this document in their entirety. Any reproduction, modification, distribution, transmission, publication, translation, display, hosting or sale of all or any portion of the contents of this document is strictly prohibited without written permission of an authorized representative of Barna Group.

The information contained in this report is true and accurate to the best knowledge of the copyright holder. It is provided without warranty of any kind: express, implied or otherwise. In no event shall Barna Group or its officers or employees be liable for any special, incidental, indirect or consequential damages of any kind, or any damages whatsoever resulting from the use of this information, whether or not users have been advised of the possibility of damage, or on any theory of liability, arising out of or in connection with the use of this information.

Unless otherwise indicated, scripture quotations are from the *New Living Translation* copyright ©1996, 2004, 2007, 2013 by Tyndale House Foundation. Used by permission of Tyndale House Publishers Inc., Carol Stream, Illinois 60188. All rights reserved.

Funding for this research was made possible by the generous support of Seed Company. Barna Group was solely responsible for data collection, analysis and writing of the report.

CONTENTS

Introduction 5
A New Sense of Missions 7
At a Glance 8

CHAPTERS

1. Communicating the Great Commission 13
   Q&A with Allen Yeh 26
2. On Mission 33
   Special Section: Experiencing the Great Commission 52
   Q&A with David Daniels 67
3. The Role of the Bible 73
   Q&A with Joyce Williams 89
4. Conclusion
   In Word and Deed 93
   5 Shifts Reshaping Missions by Mark Matlock and David Kinnaman .. 97

APPENDIX

A. Notes 105
B. Glossary 107
C. The Impact of Bible Awareness 109
D. Methodology 117
E. Acknowledgments 119
F. About the Project Partners 121

INTRODUCTION

Religious affiliation, Bible engagement, church attendance . . . Barna's business is to keep a close eye on these and other measures of faith in the United States. Over the years, we've seen some significant shifts toward a "post-Christian" environment, which we've documented in multiple reports.

Our theolographic tracking prompts questions not only about the practice of faith, but also about sharing it. In an increasingly pluralistic and skeptical culture, are people receptive to Christians who feel a burden to represent the "Good News" and make disciples? Are U.S. churchgoers even interested in this evangelistic endeavor, at home or abroad? How do pastors describe and facilitate this work? In general, as the landscape of Christianity changes, will that affect the landscape of missions as well?

Inevitably—but how, exactly? Seed Company, a ministry focused on literally spreading the gospel to all nations, came to Barna hoping to push that conversation forward. In commissioning this study, they sought to broadly understand the state of missions today and, specifically, to see how that climate influences efforts to bring scripture to every people group.

To begin the research, a brief qualitative study was conducted among 25 pastors, 31 practicing Christians and 28 churchgoing Millennials. Three surveys were then conducted in October 2017. The first study asked quantitative questions of 619 Protestant pastors (senior, lead or executive roles) in the U.S. In the second, 1,010 U.S. adults took a shorter quantitative survey. A third survey included quantitative and open-ended questions for 1,004 churchgoing U.S. adults (those who have attended a regular church service within the past six months).

The following chapters will delve into what those surveys revealed—about the U.S. Church's comprehension of the Great Commission, the current discourse surrounding evangelism and justice and, finally, the priority of presenting God's Word, in all languages. We believe this exploration is an essential aspect of the ongoing work and well-being of the global Church.

A NEW SENSE OF MISSIONS

In 2018, Seed Company celebrates 25 years of networking God's people to accelerate Bible translation. The translation of the scriptures into the heart language of the peoples of the earth is something we believe is critical to achieving the Great Commission that Jesus gave to his followers about 2,000 years ago.

Seed Company began as a new paradigm for Bible translation, addressing global shifts as we continued to bring God's Word to the world. By his grace, we have entered our 1,500th translation project in 2018. It is possible that, by 2025, no more languages will still be awaiting a translation of the scriptures, and we hope that you will "imagine zero" with us.

We partner with Christians around the globe who see faithful and accurate Bible translation as an essential step in helping churches thrive and transform their communities. But as the world—and, in turn, how we accomplish the mission of God—has changed in the 21st century, we at Seed Company have wondered what this work means to pastors and churchgoers in the United States. How does the Church in America, with its long history of missions, understand these changes?

Our hope is that the findings of this study can help pastors lead their congregations deeper into the mission of the Church, locally and globally.

SAMUEL CHIANG
President and CEO, Seed Company

AT A GLANCE

1 **Half of all U.S. churchgoers (51%) say they are unfamiliar with the term "the Great Commission."** If presented with a list of potential verses, just 37 percent recognize the correct passage that goes by this name.

2 **U.S. pastors most often define "missions" as the holistic transformation of people's lives—physical, socially and spiritually.** Churchgoers tend to describe it as verbal proclamation about the truth of Jesus Christ.

3 **Nearly half of churchgoers (46%) say "missions" and "social justice" are different but integral to each other.** Those with personal involvement in missions are more likely to see no difference between the concepts.

4 **Beyond semantics, pastors and churchgoers agree that meeting basic needs is essential in missions.** And many say physical care should take priority over or occur at the same time as spiritual ministry.

5 **The top reason churchgoers get involved in a cause is because they feel they can make a difference.** One in six credits that decision to a vision cast at their local church.

6 | **Skepticism about the intent of missions and the Bible is high among U.S. adults, especially non-Christians.** Some within the Church, especially Millennials and ethnic minorities, are also wary of missions being misused.

7 | **Three-quarters of churchgoers (75%) believe that the U.S. is better than most other countries.** Even so, a majority, especially those who travel or participate in missions, says they enjoy learning about other cultures.

8 | **Almost all pastors (95%) say growing to know, love and apply the Bible is key to transforming lives.** This aligns with churchgoers' view of scripture-reading as essential to becoming a Christian and growing in faith.

9 | **A majority of churchgoers (71%) says not having the Bible in one's own language is a spiritual barrier.** However, they consistently underestimate just how many languages and Bible translations exist.

10 | **The Great Commission's language compels churchgoers to see Bible translation as a worthwhile cause.** Nearly half see it as a fulfillment of this mandate (45%), or a way for the Church to grow through contributions of every culture (41%).

Jesus came and told his disciples, "I have been given all authority in heaven and on earth. Therefore, go and make disciples of all the nations, baptizing them in the name of the Father and the Son and the Holy Spirit. Teach these new disciples to obey all the commands I have given you. And be sure of this: I am with you always, even to the end of the age."

Matthew 28:18-20 NLT

COMMUNICATING THE GREAT COMMISSION

Jesus came and told his disciples, "I have been given all authority in heaven and on earth. Therefore, go and make disciples of all the nations, baptizing them in the name of the Father and the Son and the Holy Spirit. Teach these new disciples to obey all the commands I have given you. And be sure of this: I am with you always, even to the end of the age." Matthew 28:18—20, NLT

The passage above is the most well-known biblical record of what is commonly referred to extra-biblically as "the Great Commission," though other versions of these words from Jesus can be found in Mark 16:14–18, Luke 24:44–49, John 20:19–23 and Acts 1:4–8. In this account from the Gospel of Matthew, Jesus tells his disciples to meet him on a certain day at a certain mountain. At this post-resurrection rendezvous, Jesus delivers the command and encouragement we read in the speech above. Disciples then and now feel the weight of this instruction, which some regard as Jesus' parting words.

The phrase "the Great Commission" is believed to have first been applied to these verses by post-Reformation missionaries in the 1600s and was later popularized by missionary Hudson Taylor.[1] Throughout Church history, many (though not all) Christians have taken the passage to apply to every follower of Christ. Augustine of Hippo and Martin Bucer are among the notable names who taught that no Christians are excluded from the call to "go into all the world and preach the Good News to everyone" (Mark 16:15). The writings of Baptist missionary William Carey are perhaps most often cited for popularizing the belief that the Great Commission is an urgent calling extended to all believers, to be fulfilled internationally, and with no expiration.[2]

In the United States specifically, the First and Second Great Awakenings led to a proliferation of denominations and evangelistic missions that placed priority on the Great Commission. The mid-20th century evangelical movement also championed Great Commission language as it established parachurch missions and relief organizations, many of which focused on the concept of evangelism to "unreached people groups."[3] American churchgoers today have no lack of anthems about this idea of sharing the gospel around the world—from hymns such as "Go Ye into All the World" to modern worship songs like Hillsong's "To the Ends of the Earth" and Keith and Kristyn Getty's "For the Cause"—which they might sing on any given Sunday surrounded by church décor or banners referencing the Great Commission.

However, not all church traditions are very vocal or urgent about global disciple-making, while some of those that frequently promote missions and evangelism might not use or communicate about the phrase "the Great Commission" explicitly. Others have perhaps, if inadvertently, employed the text more like a catchphrase, rather than a command explored and fulfilled with intention. Whatever the reasons, despite the great historical, literary and biblical significance given to the verses known as the Great Commission, this study finds a surprising proportion of Christians in the U.S. is generally unaware of these famous words from Jesus.

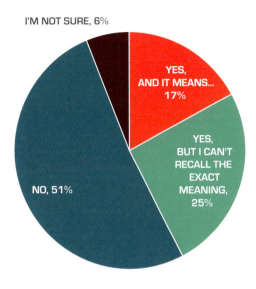

HALF OF CHURCHGOERS ARE UNFAMILIAR WITH THE GREAT COMMISSION

When Barna asked respondents if they had previously "heard of the Great Commission," half (51%) of all U.S. churchgoers (defined for this sample as those who have attended church within the past six months) said they did not know this term. It would be reassuring to assume that the other half who know the term are also actually familiar with the passage known by this name, but that proportion is low (17%). Meanwhile, "the Great Commission" does ring a bell for one in four (25%), though they can't remember what it is. Six percent of churchgoers are simply not sure whether they have heard this term "the Great Commission" before.

A little more than one-third of churchgoers correctly identifies the Bible passage known as the Great Commission

The data indicates that churches are using the phrase less, which may reveal a lack of prioritizing or focusing on the work of the Great Commission, but may also reveal that the phrase, rather than the scriptures or the labor, has simply fallen out of favor with some.

Taking a different tack, Barna also presented churchgoers with five different passages from scripture and asked them to identify which one is known as the Great Commission. (*See the following table for this collection of verses.*) A little more than one-third of churchgoers (37%) correctly identifies the Bible passage—far more than those who recognize it by its name alone. Nearly all of the churchgoers who indicate they have previously heard of the Great Commission (94%) also select the passage in Matthew 28. The remainder of churchgoers either does not know which of these verses is the Great Commission (33%) or offers an incorrect answer (31%).

Age also makes a significant difference in whether churchgoers recognize the Great Commission. More than one-quarter of Elders (29%) and Boomers (26%) says they know the text, compared to 17 percent of Gen X and one in 10 Millennials (10%). As with other churchgoing groups, people in all generations are more likely to choose the right passage from a set of options than to remember it unprompted. Roughly two in five people among the three oldest generations correctly identify the Great Commission (43% of Elders, 42% of Boomers, 41% of Gen X). Churchgoing Millennials, however, are about as likely to misidentify (36%) as to correctly identify (34%) the Great Commission. Although not even half of *any* age group knows the Great Commission well, the youngest adult generation is least likely to recognize it. Again, this study cannot conclude whether respondents are ignorant of the scriptural mandate itself, or just unaware that it is commonly called the Great Commission; in this case, it's possible older generations may be more familiar with the Great Commission because the term was previously more *en vogue* in Protestant missions.

> Churchgoing Millennials are about as likely to misidentify as to correctly identify the Great Commission

DO CHURCHGOERS RECOGNIZE THE GREAT COMMISSION AMONG OTHER VERSES?

Verse	%
"Go and make disciples of all nations, baptizing them in the name of the Father and of the Son and of the Holy Spirit, and teaching them to obey everything I have commanded you." (Matthew 28:18–20)	37%
"'Love the Lord your God with all your heart and with all your soul with all your mind,' This is the first and greatest commandment. And the second is like it: 'Love your neighbor as yourself.'" (Matthew 22:37–40)	16%
"I am the way and the truth and the life. No one comes to the Father except through me." (John 14:6)	8%
"Whoever wants to be my disciple must deny themselves and take up their cross and follow me." (Mark 8:34)	5%
"Give back to Caesar what is Caesar's and to God what is God's." (Mark 12:17)	2%
Not sure if any of these passages are the Great Commission	33%

October 2017, n=1,004 U.S. churchgoers.

Segments divide in their awareness of the Great Commission depending on denominational affiliation, church attendance, engagement with scripture and faith practice. For instance, practicing Christians (self-identified Christians who say their faith is very important in their lives and have attended a worship service within the past month) recognize the Great Commission at four times the rate of non-practicing churchgoers (25% vs. 6%).

There is a correlation between what Barna calls "Bible-mindedness"—essentially, full faith in and regular engagement with scripture—and recognizing the Great Commission. More than a third of

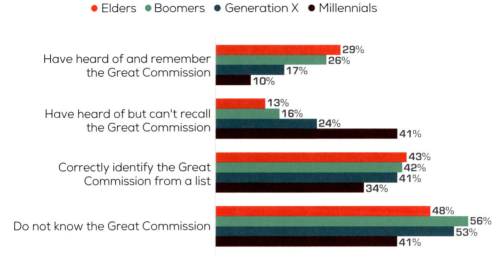

churchgoers who are Bible-minded (36%) knows the term, and over half (57%) correctly select the Great Commission from the list of possible passages. Similarly, those with higher levels of New Testament knowledge are more likely than those with less knowledge to say they know what the Great Commission is (33%) and to correctly identify it (52%). By comparison, only 1 percent of those with low New Testament knowledge are familiar with the Great Commission, and 12 percent can pick it from among other verses. (See Appendix C for details of these special Bible-minded and knowledge groups.)

Evangelicals are the most likely churchgoing group to state that they have heard of the Great Commission and remember what it is (60%), which generally aligns with their theological disposition and the criteria to be characterized as "evangelical" in the first place (An individual must meet nine criteria in order to be qualified as evangelical by Barna. See Appendix D for a full definition.). The traditional Christian views and personal spiritual commitment that shape evangelicals likely cultivate a higher level of awareness of the language of the Great Commission, and this missional jargon is more ubiquitous in the evangelical community. When selecting the Great Commission from the series of verses, three of four churchgoing evangelicals (74%) correctly identify it, the largest portion among churchgoing groups. Fittingly, American evangelicals also appear to be more Bible-minded, are more likely to be active in their churches and have deep knowledge of gospel context and the New Testament.

A survey of churchgoers' knowledge *about* the Great Commission shouldn't be conflated with an assessment of their understanding or commitment to the *spirit* of the Great Commission—a concept christened only fairly recently in Church history and concentrated most in evangelical circles. Some churchgoing groups are inevitably more likely to hear the Great Commission directly named in or connected to messages about missions. For example, 28 percent of Southern Baptist pastors and 18 percent of Baptist pastors say their last sermon about missions was specifically about the Great Commission. Non-mainline pastors (those in charismatic / Pentecostal churches, churches in the Southern Baptist Convention, churches in the Wesleyan-Holiness tradition and non-denominational churches, among others) are typically more likely than mainline ministers (those in American Baptist Churches USA, the Episcopal Church, Evangelical Lutheran Church of America, United Church of Christ, United Methodist Church and Presbyterian Church USA) to mention the Great Commission in a missions sermon (15% vs. 6%). In other words, the degree to which an individual churchgoer is personally aware of the phrasing of the Great Commission could be explained by the degree to which their own church denomination or leader publicly references it.

> Evangelicals are the most likely churchgoing group to state that they have heard of the Great Commission and to remember what it is

GRASPING THE GREAT COMMISSION

It might be surprising to learn that **half of U.S. churchgoers say they have never heard of "the Great Commission"**—the extra-biblical term for the crucial Bible passage in which Jesus commands his followers to "go and make disciples of all the nations" (Matthew 28:18-20, NLT).

So, what about those who *are* familiar?

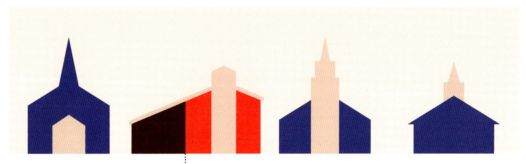

42 percent of churchgoers have heard of the Great Commission

Knowledge of the Great Commission is common among U.S. churchgoers who are:

 Has heard of the Great Commission and says they know its meaning

 Correctly identifies the passage known as the Great Commission from a list of verses

 Has heard of the Great Commission but can't recall its meaning

 Has never heard of the Great Commission

Educated |

More than one-quarter of churchgoing college graduates says they know the meaning of the Great Commission—more than three times the percentage of those with a high school education or less.

College graduates	26%	19%	46%	51%
Some college	19%	23%	40%	52%
High school or less	8%	33%	25%	52%

TRANSLATING THE GREAT COMMISSION

Elders

Churchgoing Elders know the Great Commission intimately. A lot of Millennial churchgoers are acquainted with the name only. Boomers, however, are the churchgoing age group most likely to admit *no* knowledge of the Great Commission.

	🌐	💭	✝	❓
Elders	29%	13%	43%	48%
Boomers	26%	16%	42%	56%
Gen X	17%	24%	41%	53%
Millennials	10%	41%	34%	41%

Protestant

"The Great Commission" language is decidedly more prominent in the lexicon of Protestant churches. Evangelicals are the group most familiar with the term and verse.

	🌐	💭	✝	❓
Catholic	3%	21%	18%	67%
Protestant	24%	27%	46%	44%
Evangelicals*	60%	20%	74%	19%

Engaged

Churchgoers who are involved in missions—especially those who have personally participated in it—exhibit an awareness of the Great Commission.

	🌐	💭	✝	❓
Donated to missions	22%	27%	43%	45%
Participated in missions	23%	45%	48%	23%
No involvement in missions	10%	18%	26%	66%

October 2017; n=1,004 U.S. churchgoers (those who have attended church in the past six months), 699 U.S. Millennial churchgoers
*See www.barna.com/glossary/ for the criteria Barna uses to define *evangelicals*.

THE CORE OF THE GREAT COMMISSION

The goals of the Great Commission—making, baptizing and teaching disciples of all nations—could perhaps be summarized as spiritual transformation on some level. A believer might consider this in the context of producing converts to Christianity, equipping people for long-term spiritual growth or "living" the gospel through acts of justice and service for others. U.S. churchgoers inevitably bring varying perspectives about a life of faith into their efforts to reach and teach others. Other questions in Barna's survey prompted respondents to subjectively and objectively explore some of these core ideas inherent to any discussion of the Great Commission.

MAIN FACTORS THAT POSITIVELY INFLUENCED CHURCHGOERS TO BECOME CHRISTIANS

- Growing up in a Christian family — 48%
- Attending a church service(s), other than a wedding or funeral — 38%
- An experience of the love of Jesus Christ — 33%
- Reading the Bible on my own — 28%
- A spiritual experience I could not explain — 24%
- A particular life event, whether positive or negative — 20%
- Conversation(s) with a Christian(s) I knew well — 19%
- Reading the Bible with others — 14%
- A church's outreach program (e.g., parent and toddler group, food bank, AA) — 10%
- Visiting / praying in open churches — 10%

October 2017, n=1,004 U.S. churchgoers.

When asked to name the factors that positively influenced them to personally become a Christian, the plurality—nearly half of U.S. churchgoers (48%)—says it was a result of growing up in a Christian family. Other top responses tend toward independent or intimate spiritual activities, such as attending a church service (38%), having a sense of the love of Jesus Christ (33%) or reading the Bible on one's own (28%). Corporate religious experiences, like reading the Bible with others (14%), participating in a church program (10%) or visiting an open church outside a service (10%) are less often credited for this turning point (although that doesn't mean respondents don't value them for other spiritual stages or functions).

Barna wanted to hear from pastors specifically about what they regard as most important in transforming lives for the sake of the gospel. Almost all church leaders (95%) see "helping people grow to know, love and apply the Bible" as at least "very" important, three-quarters (74%) "extremely" so. Roughly two-thirds of pastors say "helping people develop good spiritual habits, such as prayer" (65%) or "creating real opportunities for people to worship and experience Jesus" (64%) are imperative as well. Half (49%) place highest priority on "helping people develop cultural discernment (the ability to live wisely in culture today)," while 44 percent most emphasize the responsibility to "serve the poor and disadvantaged in your community." Correct doctrine isn't widely considered a core outcome of impacting others with the gospel, though about one-third of pastors still sees extreme importance in "teaching people to reject the parts of culture that do not align with biblical teachings" (31%) and "cultivating a proper, orthodox theology" (36%).

> Almost all church leaders see "helping people grow to know, love and apply the Bible" as important to life transformation for the sake of the gospel

THE CENTRAL ROLE OF SCRIPTURE

The Bible consistently surfaces in responses as a key in making and growing Christian disciples. Nearly half of churchgoers

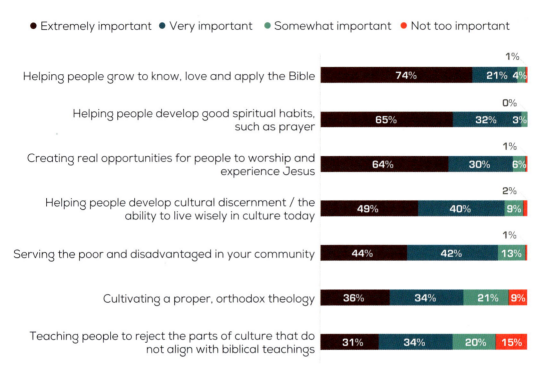

(44%) "definitely" see personally reading the Bible as an essential act in becoming a Christian, and more than a quarter (28%) names this as the biggest factor in their own journey. Evangelicals are even more likely to link scripture with this spiritual milestone, ranking solo Bible-reading (42%) second only to family influence (48%) in encouraging them to become a Christian. Most churchgoers believe that reading the Bible for themselves is also paramount in their continued discipleship (61% "definitely" + 28% "somewhat" essential), especially those who have high levels of New Testament knowledge (74%).

In other words, the Bible isn't only foundational in learning of and understanding the Great Commission; access to scripture is perceived as critical in the *whole* of the Christian life, first in choosing to follow Jesus and then in deepening, sharing and living out that decision. As such, this report will closely examine the ways American churchgoers view and value the Bible (particularly in chapter three), as well as how they think it should be positioned, communicated and translated in the global work of the Great Commission.

But first, what does that work entail, tangibly and spiritually? How is this long-held biblical directive to "go into all the world" fitting to the world's needs and mindsets today? Is it all about verbal proclamation, or tangible acts of service and aid or something in between? The next chapter explores contemporary opinions (and debates) about missions and social justice.

Q&A WITH ALLEN YEH

ALLEN YEH
Missiologist, professor, author

Allen is associate professor of intercultural studies and missiology at Biola University and serves on the Board of Trustees for the Foundation for Theological Education in Southeast Asia. His areas of geographical expertise are Latin America and China. Allen earned his B.A. from Yale, M.Div. from Gordon-Conwell, M.Th. from Edinburgh and D.Phil. from Oxford. He has been to over 60 countries to study, do missions work and experience the culture. He is also the author of *Polycentric Missiology: 21st Century Mission from Everyone to Everywhere* (IVP, 2016).

Q: A key (and some would say surprising) finding in our report is that half of U.S. churchgoers have not heard of "the Great Commission." Why do you think this is?

A: I myself am very surprised by this finding! However, the phrase "Great Commission" is not found in the Bible whereas the phrase "Great Commandment" is (see Matthew 22:35–40), so that may be part of the problem. Also, there are actually *five* Great Commissions, not just Matthew 28, which may explain part of the confusion. A "Great Commission" is the last words of Jesus to his disciples, and he gives different words in Mark, Luke, John and Acts. I think all five are worth examining.

In addition, the Great Commission is a much younger concept, historically: William Carey, the "father of modern missions," brought the Great Commission to light in 1792 through his writing of *An Enquiry Into the Obligations of Christians to Use Means for the Conversion of the Heathens*. Despite its relative "newness," I think Carey was right that the Great Commission is not a command only for the original 11 disciples (as everyone believed before 1792) but for all Christians. His rationale was that the main verb in Matthew 28 was to "make disciples." But if the original 11 made more disciples, and the Great Commission is a command to all disciples, then it must be a command for all Christians! This launched the era known as the "Great Century of Missions" (the 19th century, so dubbed by Yale historian Kenneth Scott Latourette).

I think some of the ignorance of this term can be attributed to churches not teaching this concept enough any more. I certainly heard it a lot growing up, but perhaps it has been lost on this current generation of believers. Maybe we need a new "William Carey" to revitalize interest and educate people again on it! Carey advocated for a missions conference in 1810, which never happened, but his dream came true 100 years later at the Edinburgh 1910 World Missionary Conference (the most famous missions conference in history), which lent inspiration to the triennial Urbana missions conference (where I got my call to missions when I was in college). My book *Polycentric Missiology* outlines much of the history of missions conferences since Edinburgh 1910 and their effect on mobilizing students. Historically, conferences were the things that stirred up people, and they were often aimed toward the younger generation—particularly college students, because they had education, were in the prime of their life, had much zeal and passion and were not usually married nor had children, so they were more mobile.

Q: What do you think of the loaded terms "missions" and "social justice" and the ways in which they are used in the U.S. Church today? What can church leaders do to clear some of the confusion surrounding them?
A: "Missions" is often used synonymously with "evangelism" but the two are not the same (the latter is a subcategory of the former). Missions is multi-part and includes the following: evangelism, social justice, discipleship, creation care, etc. Unfortunately, evangelism and social justice have often been pitted against each other as spiritual vs. physical ministries, respectively, representing a dualistic worldview. But in Acts 6, we see the distribution of labor of the 12 apostles (the ministry of the word) and the 7 deacons (the ministry of material things), representing caring for the whole body. So [the spiritual and the physical] should be working together and not against each other.

Our polarization of evangelism and social justice actually comes out of culture wars, not the Bible. In the fundamentalist-modernist controversy of the early 20th century, the former exclusively cared about things like the doctrine of creation, evangelism, inerrancy, while the latter exclusively cared about

"Our polarization of evangelism and social justice actually comes out of culture wars, not the Bible."

things like evolution, social justice, textual criticism. Therefore, social justice was relegated to a "liberal" issue rather than a biblical one. This was called the "Great Reversal," where conservative Christians lost social justice, so to speak. Thankfully, with the Lausanne Covenant, a social justice has been recovered as part and parcel of the holistic gospel. John Stott famously defined evangelism and social justice as two wings of a bird, or two blades of a pair of scissors: They are different, but they are equally important and they must work together. However, the fundamentalist–modernist tendencies still persist in a different form today, namely a generational divide: The older generation likes evangelism but doesn't do enough social justice, and the younger generation likes social justice but doesn't do enough evangelism. Perhaps the different generations, in dialogue with each other, can help balance each other out.

Q: **How does your experience and study speak to the importance of travel, particularly in terms of what it can teach the U.S. Church?**
A: One of my favorite quotes is by Mark Twain: "Travel is fatal to prejudice, bigotry and narrow-mindedness, and many of our people need it sorely on these accounts. Broad, wholesome, charitable views of men and things cannot be acquired by vegetating in one little corner of the earth all one's lifetime." While I love America and think that it is superior to other countries in some respects, it also pales in comparison to other countries in other respects. There are many things that I wish I could change about America to make it more efficient, more aesthetic or more logical.

On the other hand, it's certainly great to be patriotic or proud of your country for the good things. And all that is fine—there are good and bad points about every person and every country. But American exceptionalism is something that drives me crazy, and I really wish our country could have a lot more humility. If we truly believe in Christianity, then we know "how true it is that God does not show favoritism but accepts from every nation the one who fears him and does what is right" (Acts 10:34-35, NIV).

Regarding missions being misused as a way to spread Western beliefs, I think that we ought not throw out the baby with the bathwater. Rather than calling a moratorium on missions, we need to train more culturally sensitive missionaries. I know there is a lot of controversy about the value of short-term missions being "voluntourism," but I think they are great for helping the missionary learn, and also to discern whether they have a long-term call. But even if a person does not have the means (finances, time or physical ability) to go overseas, there are plenty of cross-cultural opportunities right in the midst of one's own city that can be taken advantage of.

> "Rather than calling a moratorium on missions, we need to train more culturally sensitive missionaries."

And then he told them,
"Go into all the world
and preach the Good News
to everyone."

Mark 16:15 NLT

2

ON MISSION

At the root of any conversation about the Great Commission—and suggested literally within the term itself—is the idea commonly known as *missions*. More than a quarter of churchgoers (27%) tells Barna they have participated in missions in the past year, and just under two-thirds (62%) say they have donated money to missions.

But what specifically do people mean by "missions?" It can be traced to the Latin word *mitto* and the Greek word *apostello*, both of which mean "to send."[4] But as any Christian or church leader knows, "missions" is a powerful term that is as nebulous as it is pervasive, and is rarely limited only to the individuals who are actually sent out as missionaries. Because it can often be used as catch-all for a range of evangelistic projects and outreach activities, there are a variety of definitions and approaches to modern-day missions and, as this study shows, no guarantees that U.S. pastors and churchgoers will start with the same one.

DEFINING MISSIONS

Barna's quantitative survey offered a number of possible definitions of "missions" for respondents to choose from, derived from examples and language first provided by respondents in an earlier qualitative survey. No single statement is favored by a majority of either churchgoers or pastors in the U.S.

Both groups equally regard missions as "proclaiming the truth of Jesus Christ wherever you are" (selected by approximately one in four each, and as the top choice for churchgoers). But for pastors—the individuals called and employed as spiritual caregivers—the most commonly chosen definition of "missions" (and the one that produces the biggest gap between them and churchgoers) is "the holistic transformation of people's lives by caring for their physical, social and spiritual needs" (34%), a characterization which appeals to one in five churchgoers (21%). On the other hand, churchgoers (12%) are more likely than pastors (7%) to select the one prompt that has no obvious connection to a religious vocation: "an all-encompassing word for social justice, advocacy and relief work."

> Slightly more than one in four among both pastors and churchgoers sees "missions" as "proclaiming the truth of Jesus Christ wherever you are"

WHAT "MISSIONS" MEANS TO CHURCHGOERS AND PASTORS

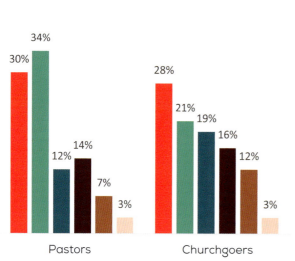

- Proclaiming the truth of Jesus Christ wherever you are
- The holistic transformation of people's lives by caring for their physical, social and spiritual needs
- The calling to proclaim the gospel to a specific people group or region
- An attitude of the heart and mind to be about the business of God
- An all-encompassing word for social justice, advocacy and relief work
- None of these

October 2017, n=1,004 U.S. churchgoers, n=619 U.S. Protestant pastors. The list of possible definitions offered here is derived from examples and language provided by respondents in a previous qualitative survey.

Non-practicing churchgoers—those who attend church but do not identify as Christian or say their faith is very important in their lives—are unsurprisingly less inclined to see evangelism as a core component of missions. One in four (25%) thinks missions should have a holistic context (compared to 19% of practicing churchgoers), while their practicing peers are more eager to see it as an opportunity to share about their faith in Christ (32%, compared to 23% of non-practicing churchgoers).

A seminary education affects how pastors define missions work. Two of five ministers without a seminary background (40%) choose "proclaiming the truth of Jesus Christ wherever you are" as the definition of missions, compared to just more than one-quarter of pastors who did attend seminary (27%). On the other hand, pastors who graduated from seminary tend to describe missions in terms of holistic transformation on physical, social and spiritual levels (37%, compared to 24% of pastors without seminary experience). Pastors who have been to seminary are also more likely to see missions as an umbrella term for social justice, advocacy and relief (9% vs. 1%).

Given the wide-ranging interpretations of "missions," Barna selected a fixed explanation for follow-up questions, encompassing ideas from the full list of possible definitions—"proclaiming the gospel and demonstrating the transformational love of Christ by caring for others and addressing their physical, social and spiritual needs"—in order to see which activities churchgoers and pastors believe fit within missions work.

While pastors are similarly aligned in the activities that characterize missions, there is a real discrepancy between newer pastors and seasoned pastors when it comes to evangelism. Pastors with at least a decade of experience (76% of those with 10–19 years, 80% of those with at least 20 years) select "sharing about Jesus with others" more often than newer pastors (59% of those with up to 9 years). Similarly, less-tenured pastors are less apt to choose any conversion activity, like "sharing your beliefs with others" and

> Pastors who graduated seminary tend to describe missions in terms of holistic transformation

CHARACTERISTICS OF MISSIONS, ACCORDING TO PASTORS' TIME SPENT IN MINISTRY

Which three, if any, of the following best fit with what "missions" is?

● 20+ years   ● 10-19 years   ● 1-9 years   ● All pastors

Sharing about Jesus with others
- 80%
- 76%
- 59%
- 77%

Doing something that benefits others
- 41%
- 44%
- 47%
- 42%

Converting others to Christianity
- 34%
- 31%
- 30%
- 33%

Having a purpose or calling to a specific cause
- 30%
- 32%
- 38%
- 31%

A period of time devoted to God through serving others
- 23%
- 33%
- 30%
- 27%

Sharing your beliefs with others
- 28%
- 28%
- 18%
- 27%

Donating money to a cause
- 7%
- 13%
- 20%
- 10%

None of these
- 3%
- 0%
- 8%
- 2%

October 2017, n=619 U.S. Protestant pastors. For this and other questions, "missions" had previously been defined as "proclaiming the gospel and demonstrating the transformational love of Christ by caring for others and addressing their physical, social and spiritual needs."

"converting others to Christianity." Instead, they prioritize more service-oriented work. Pastors who are newer to the field of ministry may be more affected by recent cultural reluctance toward evangelism and conversion, activities that could feel coercive and judgmental in an increasingly pluralistic society that, Barna research widely observes, places high value on tolerance.

Two-thirds of ministers of mainline churches (67%) say that missions is about "doing something that benefits others," even more so than "sharing about Jesus with others" (54%). Meanwhile, a large majority of pastors in non-mainline churches (87%) includes sharing about Jesus as a fitting missions activity. These opinions sync with the broader attitudes of these Protestant factions, the former stressing Christian service, the latter stressing evangelism. Like their spiritual leaders, churchgoers' perspectives on missions reflect these denominational goals. Mainline churchgoers are 17 percentage points less likely than non-mainline Protestants to say that sharing about Jesus with others fits the proffered definition of missions (69% and 52%, respectively). Meanwhile, they are 10 percentage points more likely than non-mainline Protestants to say missions should involve doing something beneficial for others (56% and 46%, respectively).

Catholic churchgoers are the least likely (43%, compared to 58% of all churchgoers) to say that missions is solely characterized by telling others about Jesus. They are also reluctant to say that missions involves "converting others to Christianity" (14%, compared to 23% of all churchgoers) or "sharing your beliefs with others" (34%, compared to 40% of all churchgoers). Instead, they gravitate toward "donating money to a cause" (25%, compared to 18% of all churchgoers) and "having a purpose or calling to a specific cause" (42%, compared to 35% of all churchgoers) as appropriate missions tasks.

In accordance with their name, evangelicals (and practicing Protestants in general) point to evangelism as a primary goal of missions, overwhelmingly selecting "sharing about Jesus with

Evangelicals and practicing Christians overwhelmingly select "sharing about Jesus with others" to describe missions work

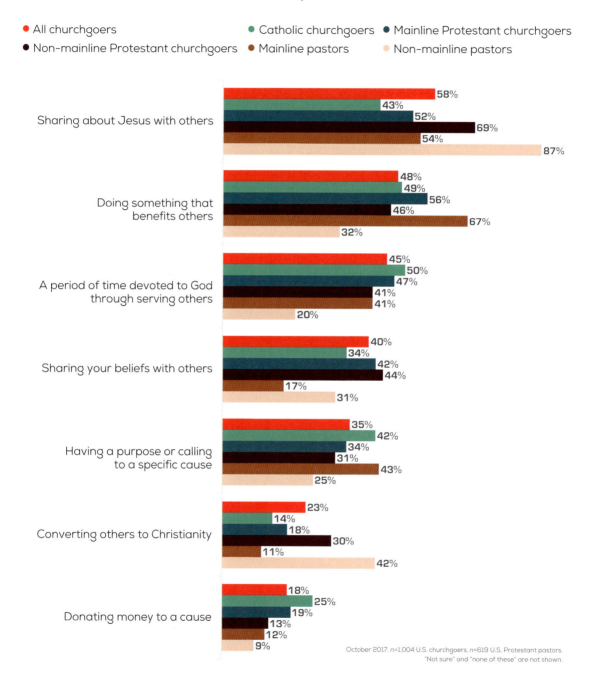

others" (86% of evangelicals and 70% of practicing Protestants). Evangelicals also choose "converting others to Christianity" at almost twice the rate of the average churchgoer (42% compared to 23%).

WHERE DOES "SOCIAL JUSTICE" FIT?

At least some of the present haziness surrounding definitions of missions is connected to either a competing or complementary understanding of social justice. To some, "social justice" can be a politically charged phrase, as in recent online memes about "social justice warriors" (or "SJWs"), a pejorative which is now defined by the Oxford online dictionary as "a person who expresses or promotes socially progressive views."[5] At the same time, there are those who use the term interchangeably with explicitly religious concepts like missions, often appealing to Micah 6:8's command to "do justice" (ESV). This see-sawing of ideas means that respondents' opinions about what social justice actually is and does are not much more conclusive than those about missions.

To Barna's sample, "social justice" usually implies a utilitarian sensitivity to "the greater good," perhaps of a more political nature because it is a term that transcends exclusively religious circles or lingo. Half of churchgoers (51%) define social justice as "promoting tolerance, freedom and equality for all people." The next most common response is that social justice means "everyone working for the common good of all" (43%). Roughly one-third describes it as "advocating on behalf of those who are less fortunate" (37%), "glorifying God through acts of justice, empowerment and love" (33%) or "seeking to right the wrongs done to others" (30%). (Totals do not add up to 100 percent, as respondents were permitted to select up to three definitions.)

The younger the respondent, the less likely they are to place a spiritual context around social justice by defining it as "glorifying God through acts of justice, empowerment and love"

> The younger the respondent, the less likely they are to place a spiritual context around social justice

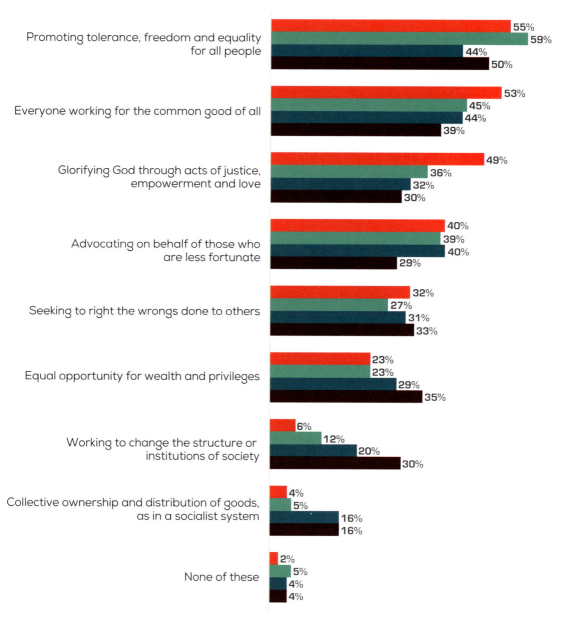

(49% of Elders, 36% of Boomers, 32% of Gen X, 30% of Millennials). This could be a result of Millennials coming of age in an era when awareness and activism have become common in social media, the marketplace, education and entertainment, and thus less confined to one segment or concept of morality. Other responses that appeal to younger respondents' ideas of social justice also have a political bent, like "working to change the structure or institutions of society" (30% of Millennials vs. 6% of Elders) or ensuring "equal opportunity for wealth and privileges" (35% of Millennials vs. 23% of Elders). The percentage of those who believe social justice hinges on "everyone working for the common good of all" follows a reverse pattern, increasing with age (53% of Elders, 45% of Boomers, 44% of Gen X, and 39% of Millennials). This "common good" language may have particular resonance for Elders who grew up in the Depression or came of age during World War II, when it was prominent in the nation's economic discussion and civilian contributions to war efforts.

With these definitions in mind, let's examine the relationship that churchgoers and pastors see between missions and social justice. Two-thirds of pastors (66%) and nearly half of churchgoers (46%) say the two efforts are different but integral to each other. Almost one-fifth of churchgoers (18%) considers social justice and missions as synonymous, more than double the proportion of pastors who view the ideas as equivalent (8%). Pastors and churchgoers are just as likely (24% each) to regard social justice and missions as two separate concepts. Tellingly, three in 10 churchgoers who report participating in missions (30%) see no difference between social justice and missions.

Along denominational lines, Catholics (23%) tend toward seeing social justice and missions as the same thing. Mainline churchgoers (21%) are more likely than their non-mainline Protestant peers (14%) to see a relationship between social justice and missions.

> Three in 10 churchgoers who report participating in missions see no difference between social justice and missions

PASTORS AND CHURCHGOERS DESCRIBE RELATIONSHIP BETWEEN MISSIONS AND SOCIAL JUSTICE

- They are essentially the same
- They are different but integral to each other
- They are distinct from each other
- Not sure

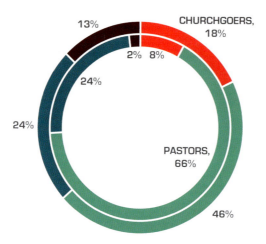

October 2017, n=1,004 U.S. churchgoers, n=619 U.S. Protestant pastors.

MISSIONS: A FIRM OR FLUID CONCEPT?

How Christians actually accomplish missions work has undoubtedly changed in many ways in the past 20 years, due to factors such as the rise of cell phone use, a global economic crisis that limited donations and missions jobs, Christianity's continuing geographical shift away from Europe and North America and toward the global South, international terrorism and more. As a result, pastors and churchgoers in the U.S. don't dispute that the general understanding or concept of missions itself has adapted in the past 20 years.

Newer pastors, with less than a decade of experience in ministry, are particularly prone to think that the concept of missions has "definitely" changed since the late 1990s (58%, compared to 46% of pastors with at least 20 years of experience and 45% of those with 10–19 years).

MISSIONS INVOLVEMENT IMPACTS VIEWS ON WHETHER THE CONCEPT OF MISSIONS HAS EVOLVED

Do you think that people's understanding of what missions is has changed over the past 20 years?

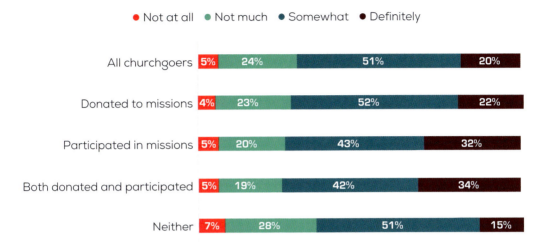

October 2017, n=1,004 U.S. churchgoers.

Seventy-one percent of churchgoers say that the popular understanding of missions has changed at least somewhat in the last 20 years. Another one-quarter (24%) acknowledges minor shifts. Only 5 percent of churchgoers think there has not been any adjustment of the public understanding of missions.

The churchgoers who are most likely to see an evolution in mindsets about missions in recent decades are those who report being involved in this work, likely because they are more personally attuned or directly exposed to possible shifts. About a third of those who have participated in missions (32% of those who have been participants, 34% of those who have also been donors) sees a transformation in the concept of missions.

Although pastors and churchgoers agree that the understanding of missions has adjusted since the late 1990s, they do not agree

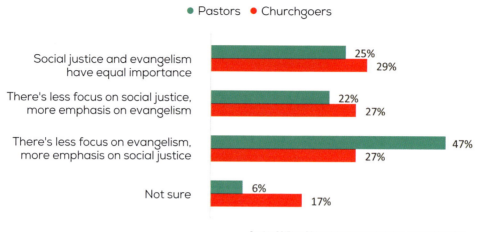

October 2017, n=1,004 U.S. churchgoers, n=619 U.S. Protestant pastors.

on what the modern approach to missions actually *is*, at least in terms of the balance of evangelism and social justice.

In describing what missions priorities are today, churchgoers' opinions don't peg one particular approach and are instead distributed among three options: that missions is now either less focused on evangelism with more emphasis on social justice (27%), or less focused on social justice with more emphasis on evangelism (27%) or equally focused on both social justice and evangelism (29%). The remaining 17 percent of churchgoers say they are not sure how to presently describe missions.

Pastors, however, have a clearer opinion of the nature of this shift: Close to half (47%) say that missions is less focused on evangelism than it used to be, with more attention given to social justice. One in four (25%) says social justice and evangelism are given equal significance now. Still, about one-fifth (22%) feels evangelism has become even more centered in missions.

A pastor's denomination also has great bearing on these responses. Three of five mainline pastors (59%) say that missions

> Close to half of pastors say that missions is less focused on evangelism than it used to be, with more attention given to social justice

has tipped toward social justice efforts and away from evangelism, compared to 42 percent of non-mainline pastors. The latter are three times more likely (28%, compared to 8% mainline pastors) to say the opposite: that evangelism receives greater attention in missions now. These responses may be representative of pastors embracing the different experiences and objectives of their own Protestant circle—mainline denominations being more focused on justice, non-mainline being more focused on evangelism—rather than observations of missions work across all denominations.

ATTITUDES TOWARD MISSIONS

Even when somebody has settled on what they regard modern missions to be, those definitions can be laden with assumptions—good and bad. Do people see this work of the Church as a worthwhile and beneficial endeavor?

When asked, "Thinking about what missions looks like today, do you think it has been a positive or negative thing for the world?" U.S. adults acknowledge mixed feelings, but a majority of the general population, and churchgoers specifically, is amenable to missions, seeing it on average as more positive than negative or even neutral. Twenty-nine percent of U.S. adults and half of churchgoers (49%) go so far as saying that it has made a "very" positive impact in the world.

Non-Christians in the U.S., however, do not share this optimistic perspective. Only 5 percent of non-Christians believe missions has "very" positive results, while just about one-fifth (22%) calls it a "mostly" positive thing. Though one in four (23%) sees missions' influence as neutral, one-third has an unfavorable impression of its impact (33% "very" + "mostly" negative).

Meanwhile, evangelicals' enthusiasm for missions continues when measuring its legacy. Three of four (75%) say missions has been a "very" positive force, and another one-fifth (21%) gives

88% of churchgoers feel missions has had a positive impact in the world

THE BALANCE OF MISSIONS AND SOCIAL JUSTICE

So, what do people mean by these terms?

Missions is …   U.S. pastors   **Social justice is …**

"the holistic transformation of people's lives by caring for their physical, social and spiritual needs"

34% — This definition is even more popular among pastors who are mainline (53%) or seminary graduates (37%)

61% — Pastors of mainly non-white congregations (81%) are especially likely to favor this definition, compared to pastors of mainly white congregations (59%)

"glorifying God through acts of justice, empowerment and love"

U.S. churchgoers

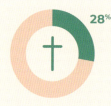 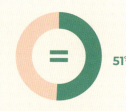

"proclaiming the truth of Jesus Christ wherever you are"

28% — This top response appeals especially to evangelicals (44%) and the highly Bible-minded* (40%)

51% — Churchgoers (51%) are in sync with all U.S. adults (57%) in holding this view

"promoting tolerance, freedom and equality for all people"

Two-thirds of pastors and **nearly half of churchgoers** say missions and social justice are different but integral to each other

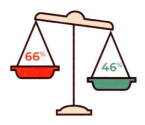

Overwhelmingly, people see missions as a force for good in the world …

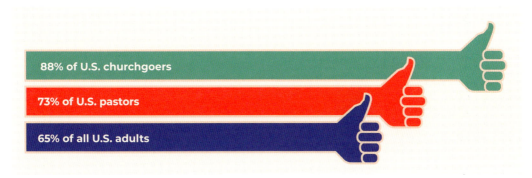

88% of U.S. churchgoers
73% of U.S. pastors
65% of all U.S. adults

and half of pastors agree the social justice movement has played a part in that.

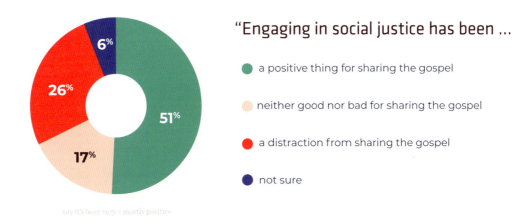

"Engaging in social justice has been …

- 51% a positive thing for sharing the gospel
- 17% neither good nor bad for sharing the gospel
- 26% a distraction from sharing the gospel
- 6% not sure

say it's been very + mostly positive

October 2017; n=1,004 U.S. churchgoers (those who have attended church in the past six months), 619 U.S. Protestant pastors, 1,010 U.S. adults.
*See www.barna.com/glossary for Bible-minded definitions.

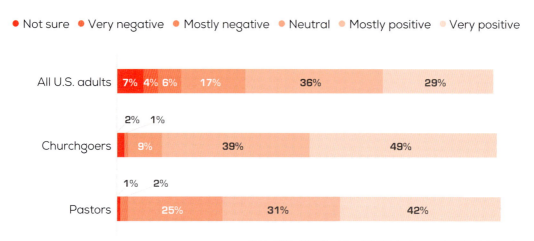

a "mostly" positive assessment. Only 3 percent of evangelicals in Barna's sample offer a neutral or uncertain assessment.

U.S. pastors are actually more reticent than their congregants to celebrate the effect of missions, and one in four (25%) has a neutral response (compared to 9% of churchgoers). It's possible that, either through on-the-job experiences or vocational training, pastors are more cognizant of potential negative impacts of missions and thus cautious of repeating Church history's mistakes. Still, three-quarters of church leaders (73% "very" + "mostly" positive) see good in missions.

The pastors who are most assured of missions' benefit to the world are those who believe it has been shifting toward evangelism and away from social justice (54% "very" positive). Notably, by comparison, just 36 percent of pastors who believe that the Church has increased its focus on social justice work are upbeat about the impact of missions. Churchgoers, however, have different takes—not only on the current balance between proclamation

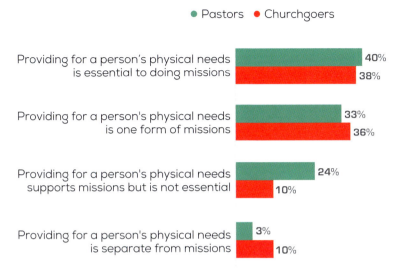

THE RELATIONSHIP BETWEEN PHYSICAL NEEDS AND MISSIONS

● Pastors ● Churchgoers

Providing for a person's physical needs is essential to doing missions — 40% / 38%

Providing for a person's physical needs is one form of missions — 33% / 36%

Providing for a person's physical needs supports missions but is not essential — 24% / 10%

Providing for a person's physical needs is separate from missions — 3% / 10%

October 2017, n=1,004 U.S. churchgoers, n=619 U.S. Protestant pastors. "Not sure" not shown.

and service, as previously described, but about how advantageous each approach may be. The majority of churchgoers who state that missions now places equal importance on social justice and evangelism sees this harmony as very positive for humanity (59%).

PRIORITIZING PHYSICAL AND SPIRITUAL NEEDS

If both physical and spiritual needs are to be addressed in achieving the Great Commission, then church assistance extends to the poor or marginalized individual who has never heard of the gospel, the believer with tangible or financial needs and the affluent non-Christian neighbor alike. Strong examples of each can be found in scripture, throughout Church history and in modern aid programs. But evolving definitions and continued debates over "social justice vs. missions" or "service vs. evangelism" are sometimes wrapped up in a fundamental Christian conflict over how to prioritize biblical responsibilities to care for the physical or

> A majority of pastors believes in addressing physical and spiritual needs at the same time

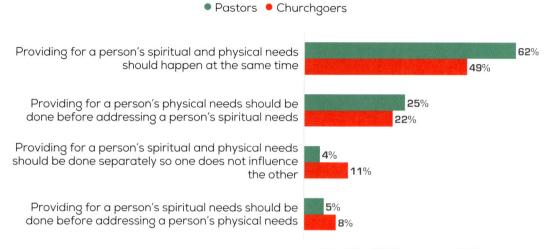

spiritual needs of others. How do the two compare or overlap, and where do they align with the work of justice and / or missions?

Pastors and churchgoers in the U.S. definitely see some connection between providing for physical needs and missions, though there is no majority viewpoint on what, exactly, that relationship is. Many—and similar proportions of pastors and churchgoers (40% and 38%, respectively)—feel that meeting physical needs is an essential aspect of missions work. One-third of pastors (33%) and churchgoers (36%) says that providing practically for a person could be one form of missions. Pastors are more than twice as likely than churchgoers to say that meeting a person's physical needs supports, but is not integral to, missions (24% vs. 10%). Though a small minority of either group separates missions entirely from fulfilling tangible needs, seeing it instead as strictly spiritual outreach, churchgoers are three times more likely than pastors to hold this distinct view (10% vs. 3%).

If significant percentages think that meeting physical needs is part of, if not crucial to, missions work, in what order do they believe the spiritual and physical aspects of missions should be addressed, particularly when both areas of need are immediate? Half of churchgoers (49%) and three out of five pastors (62%) believe in an ideal balance, addressing physical and spiritual needs at the same time. One in five churchgoers (22%) and one in four pastors (25%) say that the physical context takes precedence over the spiritual. Less popular strategies include prioritizing spiritual needs over physical ones (8% of churchgoers, 5% of pastors) or completely separating the two domains (11% of churchgoers, 4% of pastors).

It's noteworthy that pastors are even more likely than churchgoers to lean toward concrete expressions of missions. After all, pastors are seen as spiritual leaders and, as previous Barna research conducted in partnership with Pepperdine University shows, they regard spiritual instruction as their strongsuit. Yet answers to an open-ended question frequently speak of a conviction that someone must "earn the right" to broach spiritual topics only after providing physically for those in need. Pastors often echo phrasing and concepts from other spiritual leaders, like Salvation Army founder William Booth's commentary that the gospel is harder to hear over a growling stomach, or the famous words often attributed to St. Francis of Assisi: "Preach the gospel at all times. When necessary, use words." Several others allude to Teddy Roosevelt's idea that "Nobody cares how much you know, until they know how much you care."

Others look to the Bible in emphasizing the material side of missions. Of pastors who say "physical needs should be addressed before spiritual needs," a few point to scripture as their reasoning. Several respondents cite Jesus' example in arguing for the urgency of meeting physical needs. Fifteen percent of the many pastors who say "missions should focus simultaneously on the body and spirit" use the Bible to support their argument.

The rationale of some respondents paraphrases that of Maslow's hierarchy, a sociological theory which posits that physical requirements for survival make up humanity's basic and most

(Continued on page 59)

EXPERIENCING THE GREAT COMMISSION

How U.S. Churches Prioritize, Promote and Participate in Various Social and Spiritual Causes

This study, and others from Barna, show U.S. ministries are involved in a wide range of issues that could be classified as "missions," from homelessness to disaster relief, from clean water to the sanctity of life, from malnutrition to elder care. Barna asked pastors and churchgoers to identify up to three missions-related initiatives that they feel their church prioritizes. The results outline gaps between pastors and churchgoers, as well as between Protestants and Catholics (the latter often concentrate on justice work that isn't church-exclusive).

CHURCHGOERS' IDEALS VS. PASTORS' REPORTS

Barna asked churchgoers, "When it comes to donating money to or volunteering for a cause, which three of the following social issues do you think your church *should be* supporting?" Pastors were offered a similar question, with one key difference: "When it comes to donating money to or volunteering for a cause, which of the following social issues, if any, is your church *currently involved* with?" As identical options were presented to each

MISSIONS METHODS

- 83% of pastors say their churches have a budget for missions

- Half of pastors (51%) say their churches give equal attention to global and local missions

- Three-quarters of pastors (74%) say their church supports at least one missionary

- One-third of pastors (32%) says their church has heard a sermon on missions during the past month

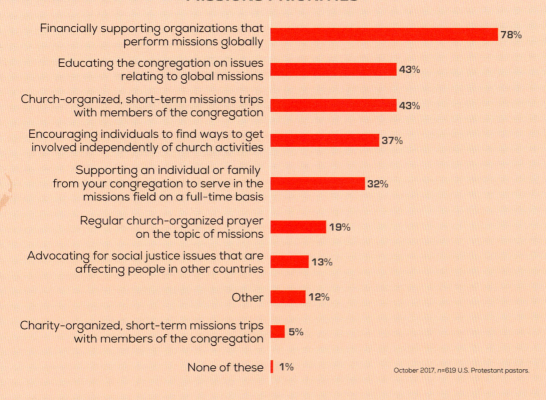

group, the researchers can compare expectations to reality and see that churchgoers' hopes for their churches' activities do not line up with the actual activities reported. For example, there is a 29 percentage-point gap between the proportion of Protestant churchgoers who think their church should support evangelism (43%) and the Protestant pastors who say their church is involved in evangelism (72%). Disaster relief, a mainstay of the missions movement, is another area in which participation (58% international, 68% domestic) far surpasses priority (14% international, 24% domestic). It's possible churchgoers' independent expectations might take a backseat to an urgent, identifiable need, such as when approached by actual missionaries or an opportunity to

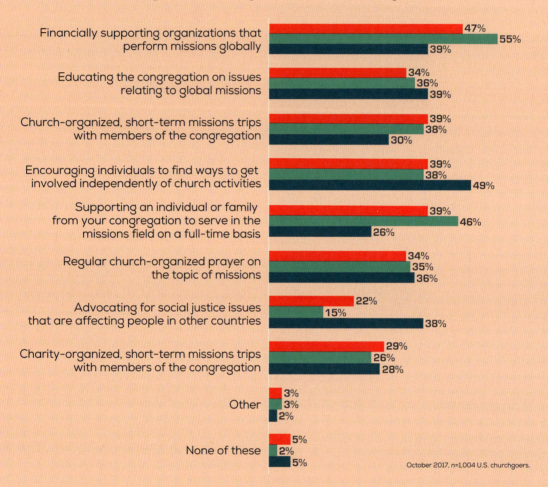

get involved in an existing project. A Barna study in partnership with Compassion International, as well as other research, suggests that specificity and immediacy often prompt interest and involvement.[6]

Generational differences stand out when churchgoers choose the top issues their church should be supporting. For instance,

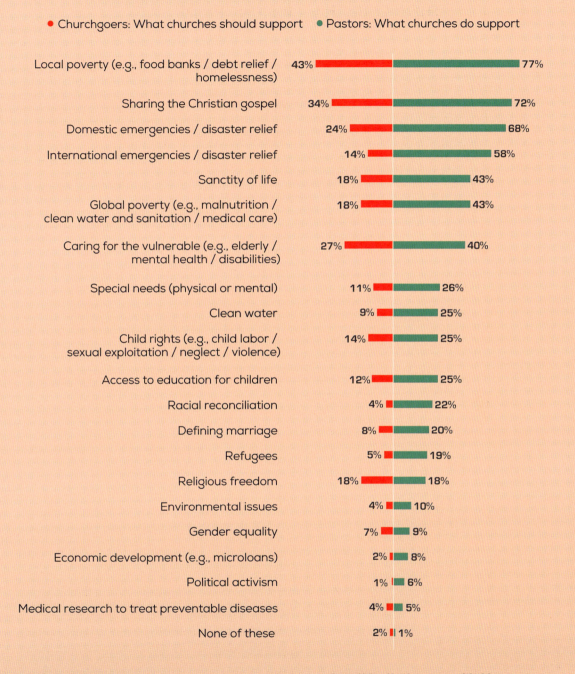

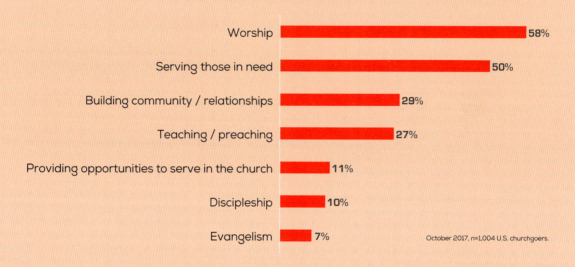

Churchgoers rank evangelism and discipleship last in a list of spiritual activities that might spur their excitement or interest

Millennials are less likely than average to prioritize local poverty (30% vs. 43% average) yet they are the age group most likely to favor child rights (18% vs. 14% average) and gender equality (12% vs 7% average). The biggest generational divide, however, pertains to evangelism; support for local church investment in evangelizing decreases with each younger age segment, producing a stark difference between Elders and Millennials (46% of Elders, 44% of Boomers, 35% of Gen X, 23% of Millennials). At the same time, Millennials are far from apathetic about the idea of missions overall; they are actually the generation most likely to report participating in related activities in the past year (39%, compared to 27% average).

It may be that some churchgoers see "sharing the Christian gospel" as something that a church could do without giving money or sending volunteers to support it, or that assistance with physical or social problems seems more urgent than spiritual outreach. Relative to other choices, funding evangelism still has

support within churches—but in absolute terms, it has only the support of a minority. Additionally, churchgoers rank evangelism and discipleship last in a list of spiritual activities that spur their excitement or interest.

TAKING OWNERSHIP

As this report shows, the current conversation about missions, social justice and everything in between has its share of ideological minefields, mixed definitions and misconceptions. But there is some common ground in motivating participation, and it's pretty hopeful: Two-thirds of churchgoers (64%) who have gotten involved in any cause, within missions or otherwise, say they did so because they felt they could make a difference. An overwhelming sense of purpose (47%) or a moving story (43%) also prompt action. Personal interactions and relationships can't be counted out; about one-third (31%) chose to participate in a cause because they personally knew someone else affected by it.

    U.S. faith communities and their regular gatherings can and should be a part of facilitating these encounters and opportunities—making the difference in helping others believe they can make a difference. After all, one in four churchgoers who has at least participated in missions (24%) or given money toward

> One in four churchgoers who has participated in or donated to missions credits that decision to a vision cast at their church

missions as well (25%) credits that decision to a vision cast at their church.

Further, strong faith informs involvement. People who are more engaged in missions are also more likely to be fully trusting of scripture. A majority of those who give time and / or money toward missions (64% who have done both, 62% who have only participated, 56% of those who have only donated) strongly agrees the Bible is accurate in all of its teachings. By comparison, 41 percent of those who have neither donated to nor participated in missions in the past year hold this conviction. Some level of engagement in missions also correlates with a firm belief that one has a responsibility to tell others about their Christian beliefs (63% of those who have both donated and participated, 60% of those who have only participated, 51% of those who have only donated), which is important to just one-third of churchgoers with no missions involvement (33% of those who have neither donated nor participated). Given these findings, it's no surprise that a high percentage of evangelicals report annual giving to missions (75%).

(Continued from page 51)

important levels of need. Many respondents refer either directly or indirectly to this assumption in putting physical needs at the forefront of missions, or at least in equal standing with spiritual service.

These responses shouldn't be solely interpreted as a belittling of the significance of spiritual missions in favor of meeting elemental human needs—and indeed, the two are not always so easily disentangled. Regardless of a pastor's approach to balancing missional engagement between evangelism and justice work, their answers are still likely to emphasize the importance of the gospel and Christians' unique position in spreading this good news. One pastor respondent writes, "The physical need will return, but the spiritual need for Christ, once met, will never return. So the spiritual need is the greater need, but that doesn't mean that the physical is dismissed or downplayed."

A GLOBAL STATE OF MIND

As Andrew Walls, a British missiologist known for his study of the African Church and of Christian history in a non-Western context, says, "Our faith is incarnational, and incarnation must always involve cultural specificity."[7] Considering this, and as the Great Commission speaks of spreading and representing one's faith to all the world, the research partners felt it was pertinent to also examine just how expansive a U.S. adult respondent's world may be. Have they traveled widely? What importance do they place on their American identity? What's their level of personal interaction with people who are unlike them? Do they appear familiar with or welcoming of other cultures and languages? And, importantly, how do these experiences or perspectives influence Christians' engagement in and thinking on missions?

Three-quarters of churchgoers (75%) agree that, "generally speaking, the U.S. is a better country than most other countries." This is just under the national average of 81 percent, though it

> Three-quarters of churchgoers agree that the U.S. is better than most other countries

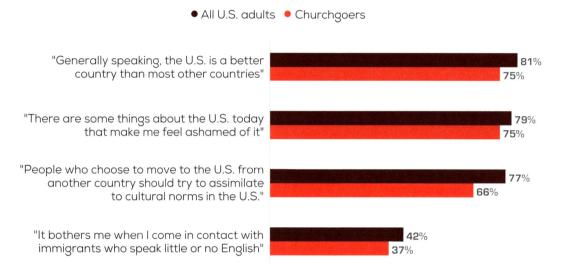

exceeds the two-thirds of non-Christian U.S. adults (67%) who feel their country is superior. It's worth mentioning here that "non-Christians" includes those of other religions, a group which often has ties to other countries, either directly or within recent generations of their family. Additionally, churchgoers of an ethnic minority, many of whom may also be able to point to a heritage from other non-Western cultures, are the least likely to agree (33% "strongly" + 33% "somewhat").

However exceptional they deem America to be, 86 percent of U.S. churchgoers still enjoy learning about other cultures at least somewhat. Practicing Catholics are the denominational group most likely to identify with this interest (60% "strongly" + 33% "somewhat"). Though a majority of practicing Protestants still expresses this idea at least somewhat, they do so less definitively (48% "strongly" + 38% "somewhat") and are on par with the churchgoing average (46% "strongly" + "40% "somewhat").

Evangelicals are the churchgoing group that is most convinced (51% "strongly" + 30% "somewhat") that the U.S. is generally better than other countries. Presumably, this viewpoint is permeated by political sentiments; conservatives make up 75 percent of evangelicals in this study and, as a whole, nearly all conservatives (92%) affirm that the U.S. is exceptional.

An openness to other cultures seems to wane when it involves interactions with immigrants in the U.S. rather than when visiting other countries. A majority of pastors (70%) and churchgoers (66%)—especially churchgoing evangelicals (78%)—agrees at least somewhat that newcomers to the U.S. should assimilate to American cultural norms. One-third of churchgoers (13% "strongly + 24% "somewhat" agree) admits frustration when they come into contact with non-English speakers. These ideas remain common even as other Barna surveys show a widespread softening in American attitudes, including across faith segments, toward immigrants and refugees.[8]

Does exposure to other nations and people groups—through specific missions or specifically through travel—impact responses to this series of questions? According to Barna's data, the short answer is yes, but not in a clear-cut way.

Nearly two-thirds of U.S. churchgoers (62%) have traveled outside the U.S. Most of those travelers went abroad more than a year ago (40% of U.S. churchgoers), and just over one-fifth (22%) made such a journey within the past year. Among the churchgoers who have been outside the U.S., the most common length of travel for a single trip is between one and two weeks (34%). About one in five (22%) has spent less than a week abroad, and an equal proportion (22%) spent between two weeks and a month away. A smaller proportion has traveled internationally for more extensive periods, up to a year (10%) or more (10%). The length

of time a churchgoer has spent abroad goes up with age, income and education—unsurprisingly, as each of these factors increases opportunity and resources to explore. Churchgoers who have traveled internationally for less than a month are more likely than those who have gone abroad for a month or more to think that the U.S. is generally better than other countries.

When churchgoers are grouped according to their investment in missions, a theme in responses is less clear. First, people who have been active in missions in the past year express more interest in other cultures. Churchgoers who have both donated to and participated in missions (63%), or those with at least one of these experiences (59% of participants, 51% of donors) tend to confidently state that they enjoy learning about people from different backgrounds. At the same time, those with personal involvement are more likely to say the U.S. is a better country than most (41% of donors and 42% of participants, compared to 32% of churchgoers engaged in neither). And, curiously, those participant groups are also more prone than those who are uninvolved in missions to feel ashamed of the U.S. (48% of those who have both donated and participated, compared to 37% of those who have done neither). Pride and shame about the U.S. may coexist in those who participate in missions, perhaps a result of a heightened awareness of the positives or negatives in other cultures.

SKEPTICISM ABOUT MISSIONS

For all of the accomplishments of Christians carrying out the Great Commission around the world, history also shows that duplication of efforts, misallocation of resources, colonialism and other issues have at times marred the efficacy and message of international missions.[9] Those sent out from the U.S. are not immune to error; returning to the words of Walls, "Among the words *American evangelical missions* the word that most people will hear first and loudest is the word *American*."[10] Further, Barna's study of the U.S., as well as the United Kingdom, shows increasing dismissal of Christianity, and its institutions and sacred texts. This particular survey probed to see if that cynicism extends to modern missions work.

Among the general U.S. population and those outside the Church, critiques of evangelism are not unusual. Significant majorities (66% of U.S. adults, 89% of non-Christians) think "it is arrogant to believe that other people or regions of the world need to assimilate to your particular faith practices." (At the other end of the spectrum, just 9 percent of evangelicals strongly agree with this statement). Forty-one percent of U.S. adults and two-thirds of non-Christians (66%) perceive that "missions today is often misused as a way to spread Western beliefs to other parts of the world."

It's not necessarily surprising that in these Church-external perspectives we see a resistance to a case for Christian missions. However, there is evidence that churchgoers too are conflicted when reflecting on missions. For example, a churchgoer may concede that missions can have adverse effects—indeed, one in four (25%) calls it arrogant to assume others should adjust to their faith practices—while simultaneously believing in a global, non-Western gospel that should be spread.

Non-white churchgoers feel some caution around the intent of missions, as their own context as an ethnic minority, perhaps even as an immigrant from another nation themselves, makes them sensitive to the harms of appropriation. Hispanic and black churchgoers, more so than white churchgoers, consider that missions can be exploited to advance Western values in other regions (21% Hispanic, 23% black, 10% white "strongly" agree) and that there is arrogance in enforcing your faith practices on other cultures (33% Hispanic, 27% black, 21% white "strongly" agree).

Millennial churchgoers, perhaps influenced by generational values of tolerance and non-intervention, are also especially wary of the potential for colonialism in missions. Half (52%) feel that missions has been misused, and more than a fifth (22%) does so strongly (compared to 13% of Gen X, 6% of Boomers and 11% of Elders).

In Barna's sample, another persistent link emerges between churchgoers who have spent more time abroad and the likelihood of believing that efforts to evangelize may have been twisted into attempts to "Westernize." For churchgoers, travel may be associated with both an appreciation of other cultures and complicated feelings about America. In this case, travel perhaps fosters respect of other cultures while also increasing chances of exposure to unfortunate examples of greedy or opportunistic evangelism in missions efforts while abroad.

That so many groups—Millennials, minorities, well-traveled individuals and undoubtedly other U.S. churchgoers—express

> Millennial and non-white churchgoers are especially wary of the potential for colonialism in missions

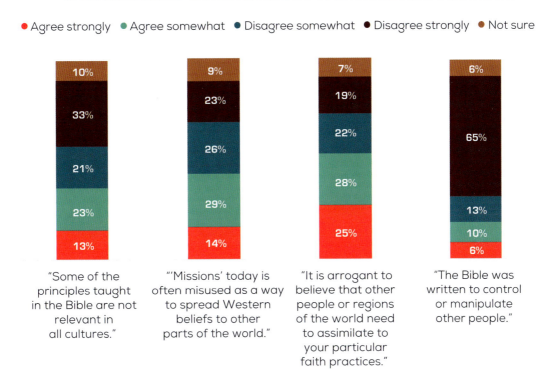

conflict over missions could pose a threat to organized missions work by discouraging people from getting involved at all. But, channeled carefully and proactively, it's an attitude that could yield deliberate and diverse missions strategies and leaders for the Church's future.

SKEPTICISM ABOUT THE BIBLE

Is there evidence of apprehension about the influence of the Bible—the source of the Great Commission and the text often regarded as central to fulfillment of missions?

Again, beyond Christian groups exclusively, there are common misgivings. Many U.S. adults (50%), especially non-Christians

(70%), hesitate to believe that biblical principles are relevant to all cultures. A quarter of U.S. adults (24%) and more than half of non-Christians (53%) go a step further, agreeing strongly or somewhat with perhaps the most damning perspective on Christianity in the survey: "The Bible was written to control or manipulate other people."

Though more than a third of churchgoers (36%) doubts that some biblical principles have a meaningful place in all cultures, they draw a firm line in disagreeing that the Bible is a tool intended to manipulate other people (65% "strongly" + 13% "somewhat" disagree). Practicing (81%) and evangelical Christians (96%) are even more opposed to this characterization of scripture. Ethnicity, again, has some bearing on responses; Hispanic (26% "strongly" agree) and black (19% "strongly" agree) churchgoers recognize cultural limits to some biblical conventions, and the Hispanic segment particularly questions if the Bible has potential to manipulate people (17% "strongly" agree, vs. 9% black and 6% white churchgoers).

One solution offered to these often legitimate concerns about appropriation and arrogance in U.S. missions is Bible translation. If the presence of scripture is foundational to the calling and work of missions, having scripture in *every language* helps to address critiques of missions, by aiding the spread of the gospel with respect to the agency and culture of each individual. In the following chapter, Barna asks churchgoers and pastors about their knowledge of the process and purpose of Bible translation and their interest in this empowering manifestation of the Great Commission.

Q&A WITH DAVID DANIELS

Q: What do you feel pastors' approach should be in communicating about the Great Commission (as a verse, concept and mission)?

A: Some churches view mission and evangelism as "one item on a spiritual buffet." That is, the Great Commission is one of many options for churchgoers who feel personally inclined. Other churches view mission and evangelism as "one item on a spiritual plate"—like beets, the Great Commission doesn't appeal to most people, but everyone has to eat their vegetables, so to speak. Both of these distorted views fail to put gospel proclamation as the centerpiece of the Church's existence. David Bosch rightly states in his book *Transforming Mission*, "There is a church because there is a mission, not vice-versa." When pastors think exclusively about the gospel as God's means for serving people instead of the Church's motivation to serve the world, the Great Commission gets lost in the flurry of church-centric activities. The Great Commission and the glory of God it declares must be more than a verse; it must be the driving force of a disciple-making church.

Q: What can pastors do to make biblical study more central in their ministry and in the lives of those they lead? How does this extend to missions work as well?

A: People who don't open their Bible have an opinion of scripture that is either too low or too high. The pastor can help their people know, live and apply the Bible by first elevating scripture and showing its beauty. This means that they preach *biblical* truth, not just truth, in the pulpit. They help their people see the logical connection of a text to their personal lives.

DAVID DANIELS
Pastor, author

David has served as lead pastor of Pantego Bible Church in Fort Worth, Texas since 2005. He has a B.F.A. from the University of Texas at Austin, a M.Div from Denver Seminary and a D.Min from Dallas Theological Seminary. David is co-founder of Beta Upsilon Chi (Brothers Under Christ), a national Christian fraternity. He has been on short-term missions to Cuba, Dominican Republic, India, UAE, Burundi, Rwanda, Ethiopia, China, Spain, Russia and Ukraine. David's teaching and training ministry includes the *Perspectives on the World Christian Movement*, Pine Cove Christian Camps and Kanakuk Institute. He is author of *Next Step Discipleship* and *Next Step Church*. David and his wife, Tiffany, live in Arlington, Texas and enjoy life with their children, Grant (and his wife, Laine), Pearson and Jenna.

They unpack the complexities of scripture to reveal a book that is a divine masterpiece instead of an ordinary, human work. They train, counsel, marry and bury on the foundation of God's Word so that their people learn that scripture is food for life (Jeremiah 15:16).

At the same time, the pastor can demystify scripture to show its accessibility to all. The Bible was written not to be understood only by the educated scholar, but by every person who has come into community with the living God. God speaks in a way that all of His children may understand. When people begin to grow through self-discovery, the Bible becomes brighter and more alive to them.

Because God is a personal God, people encounter God best when He meets them personally—speaking *their* language, in *their* place, making sense of *their* unique circumstances. Through stories, statistics and personal example, we have tried to help people understand the power of God who speaks through His Word, not "generally," but specifically *to me*.

> "People encounter God best when He meets them personally—speaking *their* language, in *their* place, making sense of *their* unique circumstances."

Q: Among churchgoers, groups including Millennials, ethnic minorities and those with more international travel experience are some of those who face a sense of wariness toward missions and a concern about it being misused at the expense of other cultures. How can church leaders hear, respond to and harness these attitudes in their congregations?

A: Delivering the gospel of Jesus is fundamentally a rescue mission—people who are safe helping people who are in need. The Christian cannot avoid the reality that they know "the Way." Still, those committed to gospel mission must resist any appearance of American, white or Western supremacy as they reach across cultural boundaries. This begins, I believe, in the way a church treats various cultures in its own backyard. Churches who celebrate cultural, ethnic, economic and educational diversity are less likely to develop an "us vs.

them" mentality. Pastors can affirm the dignity of all people by telling stories where international friends are the heroes rather than helpless recipients. Building partnerships with international organizations that understand local cultures and cooperating with indigenous leaders to direct ministry initiatives rather than importing pre-packaged ministry plans help greatly. And, in an age when social media is often the best communication, travelers should avoid pictures and posts that unintentionally exploit people and places as proof that we are "doing a good thing."

Then he opened their minds to understand the Scriptures. And he said, "Yes, it was written long ago that the Messiah would suffer and die and rise from the dead on the third day. It was also written that this message would be proclaimed in the authority of his name to all the nations, beginning in Jerusalem: 'There is forgiveness of sins for all who repent.' You are witnesses of all these things. "And now I will send the Holy Spirit, just as my Father promised. But stay here in the city until the Holy Spirit comes and fills you with power from heaven."

Luke 24:45-49 NLT

THE BIBLE'S GLOBAL ROLE

The Bible was originally written over many centuries in Hebrew, Aramaic and Greek, but as those tongues fell into disuse, scripture was translated into more contemporary languages. After the last western Roman Emperor (during the period often referred to as the Dark Ages), the Bible was translated into Chinese, several Central and Eastern European languages and Arabic. Languages such as French, Czech, Hungarian, Russian, German, Spanish and Finnish received Bibles during the medieval period.[11] The first complete translation of the Bible into an English language, an effort led by John Wycliffe, was published in 1382.[12] This particular Middle English form, translated from the Latin Vulgate, preceded the popular "authorized" King James Version by several centuries.[13]

Near the time of the Reformation, there was a burst of Bible-translating activity, linked not only with Christianity's growing autonomy beyond the Catholic Church but also the invention of the printing press and a subsequent increase of literacy. Most known translations at that time were by Europeans into their mother tongues (or "heart language").[14] While some Bible translation work was happening in Africa and Asia, William Carey's missionary movement of the late 1700s began to accelerate Bible translation across India and beyond, specifically as an endeavor positioned within the Great Commission calling.[15] In the first 1,800 years of the Christian Church, 70 languages received Bible translations; by comparison, in the 19th century alone, 460 more translations were completed.[16]

Twentieth century missionary William Cameron Townsend, of Arkansas, founded several programs to make scripture accessible to minority language groups, including a training camp that would eventually become the organization Wycliffe Bible Translators. His work is said to have sparked the modern Bible translation movement as we know it.[17]

More recently, ethnodoxology, the study of how different cultures worship through music, is making related strides alongside Bible translation in ensuring people groups also have Christian songs that center their own languages, melodies and artistic styles.[18] Such missions focuses—distinctly evangelical, anthropological and educational—have positive outcomes beyond the apparent spiritual ones, like encouraging literacy, alleviating poverty, elevating marginalized cultures or preserving endangered languages. "When we translate scripture into the heart language of people who do not have a written language, we are empowering them to read the Word of God, to hear the story of how much they are loved and made in the image of God," Reverend Dr. Brenda Salter McNeil says, "but we are also empowering them to read, to be educated and to become fully functioning citizens in their society."[19]

BIBLE TRANSLATION IN MISSIONS

As mentioned earlier in this report, U.S. respondents recognize the Bible as a powerful force for personal spiritual growth. A majority of churchgoers reports engaging with the Bible on their own, and frequently; 55 percent report some amount of weekly Bible-reading (20% every day, 9% four or more times a week, 16% several times a week, 10% once a week), for an average (median) of 30 minutes in a single reading.

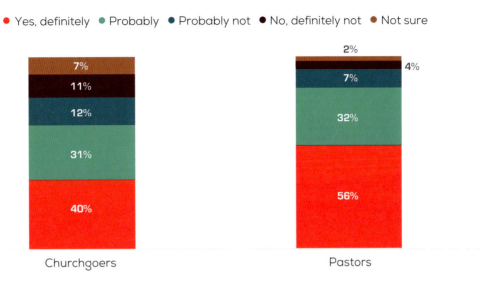

American churchgoers not only read the Bible; they also look to it for truth. A majority agrees (51% "strongly" + 31% "somewhat") that scripture is totally accurate in all of the principles it teaches. Churchgoers who know more about gospel context are even more likely to claim this view and to say that their faith is important in their lives today.

If U.S. churchgoers are so devoted to the Bible for themselves, do they see the translation of scripture into other languages as its own mission, fundamental to carrying out the Great Commission and making disciples of all nations? Seven in 10 churchgoers (71% "definitely" + "probably") believe that not having the Bible translated into one's native language can be a barrier to becoming a Christian. Pastors (88% "definitely" + "probably") are even more convinced of the urgency of scripture translation in helping others to become Christians

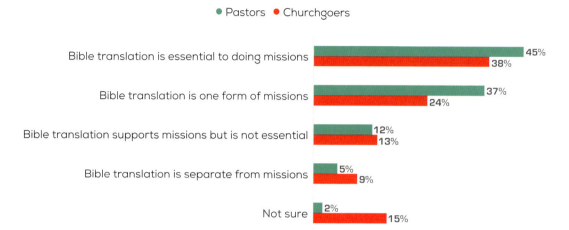

> More than one-third of churchgoers and close to half of pastors say Bible translation is truly essential in the success of missions

Smaller proportions of churchgoers (38%) and pastors (45%), however, say Bible translation is truly *essential* in the success of missions. Others consider it one form of missions (24% of churchgoers, 37% of pastors) or see it as an act of support for other missions work (13% of churchgoers, 12% of pastors). Small percentages of each group (9% of churchgoers, 5% of pastors) don't see a connection between Bible translation and missions. Pastors are somewhat more likely than churchgoers to esteem Bible translation as a missions aim. Fifteen percent of churchgoers simply aren't sure what to think.

Evangelicals are the most likely group to say that Bible translation is essential to missions (61%), followed by practicing Protestants (49%). The more familiar a churchgoer is with the New Testament, the more likely they are to say that Bible translation is essential to doing missions (45% of those with a high level of knowledge, 38% with a medium level of knowledge, 27% with a low level of knowledge).

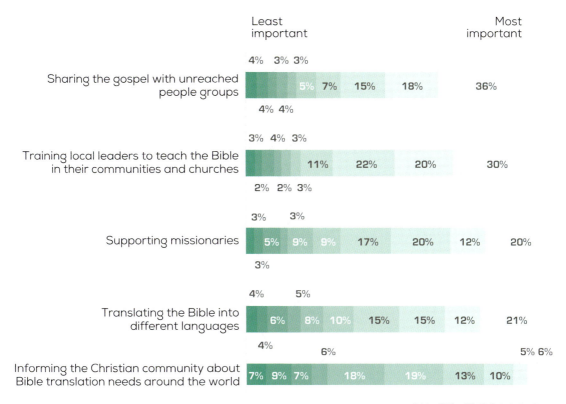

The most significant factor in saying that Bible translation is essential to doing missions is Bible-mindedness. When travel experience, income, age and education level are controlled for, analysis shows the more Bible-minded a churchgoer is, the more likely he or she is to see translation as indispensable. Similarly, Bible-mindedness has a statistically significant effect on whether someone sees Bible translation as supportive but non-essential to missions—but this time in reverse: The less Bible-minded someone is, the more likely they are to agree with this option. Even experience with travel does not seem to drastically change the way average churchgoers see Bible translation's relationship to missions.

When presented with a brief list of related ways to conduct missions, Bible translation does not presently emerge as a key focus for U.S. pastors. Even so, more than a third of pastors (36%) sees sharing the gospel (presumably, primarily verbally) with unreached people groups as the most important. This is followed by training locals to lead spiritually in their communities, supporting missionaries and then translating the Bible into other languages.

RESPONDENTS EXPLAIN THEIR OPINION OF BIBLE TRANSLATION

The survey offered an option to write in one's argument for selecting a particular view of Bible translation in relation to missions. For one-third of U.S. churchgoers who say that Bible translation is necessary in missions, the common rationale is that having access to the Bible in one's own language leads to better understanding and application of God's word. One in five churchgoers sees Bible translation as a missions essential because all languages deserve and need to have a Bible in their language. One churchgoer says, "The Holy Spirit came down in Acts so every man could understand in his own language, so why would every man not deserve to understand today?" Another Millennial churchgoer expresses concern about people being unable to make direct comparisons between the Bible and what they've been taught about it: "In order to speak about the Word, the Word needs to be within reach of all who are hearing. Otherwise, the one teaching can say anything they like and no one would be able to prove them right or wrong."

Half of U.S. pastors who say that Bible translation is essential to missions reason that having an accessible, understandable Bible makes it possible to truly know God and the gospel. A quarter points to people's ability to grow spiritually through personal study when there is a Bible they understand.

Half of pastors who say that Bible translation is essential to missions reason that it makes it possible to truly know God and the gospel

Churchgoers who say Bible translation is just a method of supporting rather than accomplishing missions give a wide variety of reasons. Some say that hearing about, rather than reading from, the Bible in one's own language is enough. Others return to an idea covered at length earlier in this report: that provision for physical needs should come before Bible translation, a spiritual need. A minority writes that the Bible and its content are simply unnecessary for missions or ministering to others. Many of these viewpoints seem either to focus on the very beginning of a person's Christian life or to depend on extra-biblical spiritual instruction and discipleship. "I think the Bible should be optional on missions," one churchgoer says. Another states, "It is still possible to meet someone's physical and spiritual needs without a translation of the Bible."

Pastors who also view Bible translation as just a useful reinforcement to missions offer similar reasoning. A slight majority posits that as long as the gospel is conveyed in some manner, missions can be conducted without an appropriate translation of the Bible. Several pastors say that the Christian message is better seen than heard anyway. The same proportion of pastors says Bible translation is not essential because it was not a part of the growth of the early Church, when oral scripture was still the standard and completed manuscripts and a New Testament were still to come. Elsewhere, pastors advocate for a continued oral tradition today, where laypeople learn from the Bible indirectly via a pastor or preacher.

When Bible translation is regarded as one form of missions, it's likely because it's seen as a sort of specialty pursuit, like medical missions (mentioned by nearly half of this group). Sixty percent of pastors who chose this option often indicate that missions could involve many goals and approaches, including Bible translation. The reality is that modern U.S. missions efforts may focus on reaching the groups who *do* already have a Bible translation—roughly 80 percent of the global population has access to scripture in their first language[20]—and thus other forms of physical and spiritual service are an established priority.

Behind the idea that Bible translation is completely separate from missions is the assumption that translation is not always necessary (an idea referenced by a few of those who see translation as non-essential). Others reiterate that the gospel could be shared through actions rather than words. One churchgoer selects this option because of a solely verbal definition of missions: "Preaching is missions. Translating is just putting the words in context and language of the people." Others object to translation as an opportunity for "telling others what to believe" or assume that "the Bible has already been translated" and further translation work is not required.

Throughout responses, a common theme is the belief that the Bible itself is not foundational to Christians' mission or message, especially when other social or physical needs are also apparent. Other U.S. churchgoers and pastors expressed ideas including: "God's words do not feed or clothe people." "No need to proselytize needy people." "God wants us to love and care for each other, and you don't have to have the Bible translated to show and teach that." "Missions show our acts of kindness and how religion and Jesus have shaped our lives. It is through acts and deeds rather than preaching that [we] will change a person's view and possibly life. Actions speak louder than words."

WHAT PEOPLE KNOW ABOUT BIBLE TRANSLATION

The methods of Bible translation have inevitably evolved, expanded and improved with time. Today, Bible translation involves a team, including scholars, often from the relevant region themselves, with knowledge of linguistics, sociolinguistics, anthropology, literacy and translation. The common model is locally defined, shaped by the needs of indigenous churches and contributions of mother-tongue speakers, with the support of ministry partners and advisement of expatriate missionaries.[21]

Bible translation is apparently pretty familiar to most U.S. churchgoers; only one of seven (14%) says he or she is wholly unfamiliar with the subject or process. So where are people learning about Bible translation? There is no single resource cited by a majority, though several (30%) remember hearing about Bible translation at church in a sermon. Other churchgoers gleaned information about Bible translation at a Bible study or small group (21%), at church in a class setting or Sunday school (20%), in conversations with friends and family (15%), other Christians (15%) or a church leader (11%).

Despite reporting a certain level of awareness about translating the Bible into other tongues, some blind spots remain. For example, neither pastors nor churchgoers are very familiar with the number of languages in the world, let alone how many have a Bible translation. Though it's difficult to report with precision just how many global languages exist—humanity continues to surprise itself, discovering previously unknown people groups and vocabularies—an estimate from Wycliffe Bible Translators supposes that the complete Bible is currently available in at least 600 of the world's 7,000+ languages said to be in use today, a proportion amounting to about 9 percent. For another 1,600 or so languages, a Bible translation exists at least in part, often just a New Testament. Excluding sign languages, unviable dialects or the 2,584 languages for which translation and linguistic development work is in progress, roughly 1,600 spoken tongues still await any Christian scripture translation project.[22]

Most churchgoers' answers consistently come in below these estimates. The most common guesses reach from 50 to 500 languages, with an average estimate (median) of 100 languages in the world. Some churchgoers give numbers wildly outside of this range, up to 500,000. Likewise, churchgoers' estimates of the number of Bible language translations fall short, between 20 and

> Neither pastors nor churchgoers are very familiar with the number of languages in the world, let alone how many have a Bible translation

200 with an average of 50. Seventeen percent of churchgoers assume there is no work left to be done in this area, guessing incorrectly that *all* of the world's languages have a Bible translation.

The average American pastor's answers are slightly closer to reality than churchgoers'. Nine percent correctly assume there are 6,500–7,500 languages in the world, compared to the median guess of 2,000. A similar proportion (11%) suggests the right number of existing Bible language translations.

HISTORICAL AUTHORITY OF THE BIBLE

Tangential to one's assessment of the importance of Bible translation is an evaluation of the credibility and accuracy of the Bible, particularly as it has expanded in interpretations and translations over time. What, if anything, do people cling to as sacred or immutable in scripture?

CHURCHGOERS ON THE NATURE OF THE BIBLE

● Original text   ● Translated texts

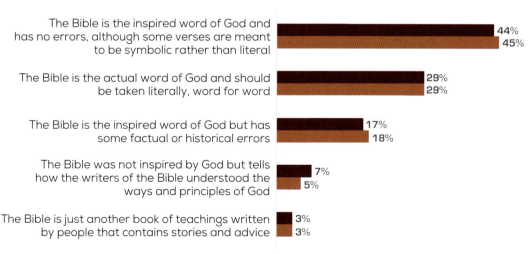

The Bible is the inspired word of God and has no errors, although some verses are meant to be symbolic rather than literal
- 44%
- 45%

The Bible is the actual word of God and should be taken literally, word for word
- 29%
- 29%

The Bible is the inspired word of God but has some factual or historical errors
- 17%
- 18%

The Bible was not inspired by God but tells how the writers of the Bible understood the ways and principles of God
- 7%
- 5%

The Bible is just another book of teachings written by people that contains stories and advice
- 3%
- 3%

October 2017, n=1,004 U.S. churchgoers.

THE WORLD OF BIBLE TRANSLATION

And what U.S. churchgoers (don't) know about it

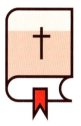

Seven in 10 churchgoers in the U.S. believe that not having the Bible in one's native language can be a barrier to becoming a Christian—but they lack an understanding of the scope of translation work. Meanwhile, roughly **220 million** people still await access to scripture in their own tongue. Here's an overview of the current state of Bible translation.

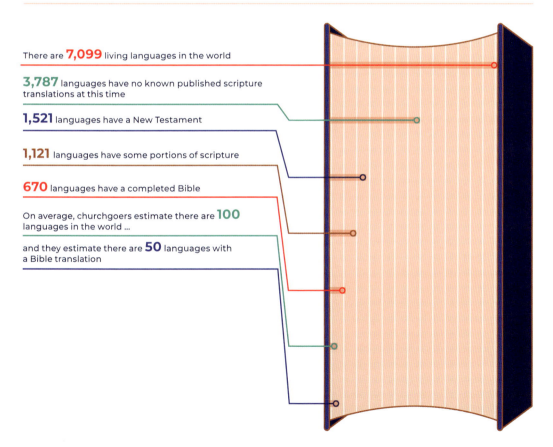

There are **7,099** living languages in the world

3,787 languages have no known published scripture translations at this time

1,521 languages have a New Testament

1,121 languages have some portions of scripture

670 languages have a completed Bible

On average, churchgoers estimate there are **100** languages in the world …

and they estimate there are **50** languages with a Bible translation

October 2017, n=1,004 U.S. churchgoers. Additional Source: Wycliffe Global Alliance, October 2017

About half of U.S. adults believe the Bible in both its original text (51%) and English translations (48%) are the word of God and are without error. Unsurprisingly, churchgoers are even more likely to think so, with nearly three-quarters saying that both the original (73%) and later translations (74%) are the inspired word of God and faultless. Interestingly, though, they might not know much about how that original text came to be: When presented with a list of 11 languages and asked to identify the ones in which the Bible was initially written, just one in 20 churchgoers (5%) correctly selects versions of Hebrew, Aramaic and Greek.

Similar proportions of U.S. adults, churchgoers and pastors believe that the Bible is the inspired Word of God but with *some* factual or historical errors. About one in five speaks this way of the original scriptures (18% of U.S. adults, 17% of churchgoers, 21% of pastors) and subsequent translations (20% of U.S. adults, 18% of churchgoers, 29% of pastors).

Of the three main survey groups, pastors are actually most likely to assert that the divinity and accuracy of biblical texts have changed or been called into question over time. A greater proportion of pastors describes the Bible in its original form (75%)—rather than the current translations they use today (60%)—as the inspired word of God with no errors. A fifth (21%) allows that the original Bible, though still inspired by God, has some errors, a proportion that increases (29%) when looking at their present translations of the Bible. Half of pastors (50%) propose that, once translated, scripture is increasingly meant to be read symbolically, rather than literally, while 10 percent say it can no longer be described as inspired directly by God.

BIBLE TRANSLATION'S VALUE, ACCORDING TO NON-ENGLISH SPEAKERS

In the absence of Bible translations in every mother tongue, does a language barrier present a potential spiritual or theological barrier? There is some evidence that knowledge of scripture in a majority language does not guarantee a deep understanding of Christianity in one's heart language. For instance, in one study among the Bajju in Nigeria, where churchgoers were taught in Hausa instead of their mother tongue, one in five could not appropriately answer the question "Who is Jesus?"[23]

Barna asked ESL (English as a second language) speakers in its sample—who make up 21 percent of U.S. adult churchgoers—to respond in writing to the question, "How might it affect your faith if you were unable to read the Bible in your first language?" Approximately a third of churchgoing ESL speakers says that the Bible would be more confusing if it were not in their native language. Some indicate that they would not be able to study the Bible on their own without a translation. One churchgoer says that if the Bible were not in his native language, "I probably wouldn't have read it." "I wouldn't be able to

> Approximately a third of churchgoing ESL speakers says that the Bible would be more confusing if it were not in their native language

connect to the Bible and Jesus' teachings if I didn't understand the passages fully," writes another.

Millennial ESL churchgoers highlight another factor: Not having a Bible in one's native language can lead to bad interpretations. Without a native language translation, one says, the only option is "trusting what other people are saying."

Just behind Millennials is Generation Z, a group that is both the most diverse and most post-Christian generation the U.S. has yet seen, according to a Barna study in partnership with Impact 360 Institute. The above concern highlighted by their ESL peers—that Bible translation allows for non-English speaking individuals to have a sense of agency in their Bible study—aligns with teens' desires for evidence to back up their beliefs. For younger churchgoers especially, a Bible in one's own hands and own tongue speaks to more than one felt need.

Some ESL churchgoers in the U.S. are not so concerned about the lack of a scripture translation in their first language, since they do have access to one they can understand in English or are taught by pastors they trust. Twenty-three percent say that it would not be an issue. Some are content to learn about the Bible secondhand from priests or preachers. "I haven't read a Bible in my first language. I just simply attend church and learn from there," writes one respondent. One Millennial ESL churchgoer feels that not having a native language translation would have "no effect at all," adding that their "faith in God is not about the Bible."

REASONS TO TRANSLATE

Given the moderate awareness of and support for Bible translation within missions, what might make a convincing argument for support of this initiative? Barna suggested a number of possible reasons that Bible translation could impact or appeal to communities. Similar majorities of U.S. churchgoers gravitate toward a series of options that elevate the individual's spiritual experience and agency: Translating the Bible into a person's own language "shows that the Bible is for everyone" (58%); "shows Christ to them in their own terminology" (55%); and "empowers people to take ownership of their spiritual education and growth" (54%).

Almost half (45%) see Bible translation as a very convincing cause when it's framed within the language of the Great Commission, as "a fulfillment of the mandate to all Christians to share the gospel." A similar proportion feels that *everyone* has something to gain from Bible translation—that it could be important because "the Church as a whole is able to mature through the contributions of every individual and culture" (41%). A majority of evangelicals and practicing Protestants finds these arguments based in a biblical mandate (60% evangelicals, 58% practicing Protestants) and maturing the global Church (55% each) to be compelling reasons to support Bible translation. As one churchgoer writes, "Access to the Bible in a person's heart language is a powerful tool for evangelism and discipleship."

The late theologian and African missiologist Dr. Kwame Bediako expressed something similar: "Here we get to the heart of the Great Commission—the discipling of the nations—the conversion to Christ of all human cultural worlds, the things that make people into nations, the shared processes of thought and conduct and their penetration by the mind of Christ. For, as Christ becomes incarnate in each cultural context, so new dimensions of Christ himself are revealed for the benefit of the world church."[24]

> Almost half of churchgoers see Bible translation as a very convincing cause when it's framed within the Great Commission

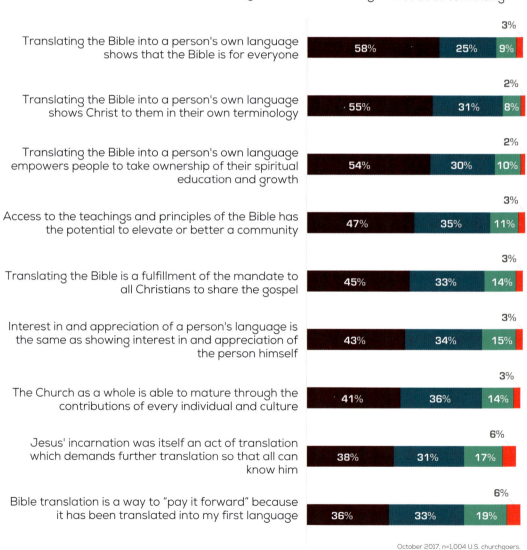

Q&A with JOYCE WILLIAMS

Q: What do you think of the loaded terms "missions" and "social justice" and the ways in which they are used in the U.S. Church today? What can church leaders do to clear some of the confusion surrounding them?

A: Historically, "missions" has been understood as the spreading of the gospel throughout the world. Many subcategories would fall into missions: evangelism, leadership development, discipleship, church planting, Bible translations, medical missions . . . the list goes on and on. "Social justice" is a relatively new term in the arena of Christian missions. Human rights issues surrounding slavery, clean water, human dignity and serving the poor have surfaced as important areas in which the Church should be very active. I consider social justice issues to falls into the subcategory of missions. The worldwide Church should be the hands and feet of Christ, serving all the needs of all people in their community.

Q: What do you see as the function or role of scripture in missions work? Is the presence of the Bible (particularly in a heart language) essential, and if so, what changes might it prompt?

A: I am convinced that scripture in one's heart language is the key that unlocks one's understanding of the person of Jesus Christ. Scripture is both simple and complex. It teaches in parables and stories and is therefore best understood in the language that one knows best, their heart language. Translating the Bible into the heart languages also allows the less educated to have access to the scriptures because they may not understand their own national language. Once the scripture is translated, Truth enters into a community. It breaks

JOYCE WILLIAMS
Chairwoman of the Board for Seed Company

Joyce has multiple years of board governance experience with Cornerstone Trust, The Gathering, Gull Lake Ministries and is the current chairwoman of Seed Company. Involvement in the developing world has offered her the opportunity for extensive international travel. For more than 10 years, Joyce worked as a staff member with Young Life and volunteered on its local committees. Joyce and her husband, Ron Williams, live in Grand Rapids, Michigan. They have four grown children and 11 grandchildren.

the bonds of sin and corruption and teaches us to love and forgive one another. Its message is powerful.

Q: About four in 10 pastors and churchgoers in the U.S. say that meeting physical needs is essential to doing missions. Twenty-five percent of pastors and 22 percent of churchgoers say physical needs should actually come first, before spiritual needs. Based on your work, how would you speak to this balance? What could the Church uniquely bring to each realm of aid?
A: The Church around the world is best equipped to meet both the physical and the spiritual needs of their local communities. They have the ability to give a cup of cold water to those in need, but they are also available to offer living water, water that will quench one's thirst forever (John 4:13–14). It should not be one or the other; it needs to be both. The church is naturally positioned to share God's message of love and to care for the physical needs of those around them.

Again he said,
"Peace be with you. As the Father
has sent me,
so I am sending you."

John 20:21 NLT

CONCLUSION

IN WORD AND DEED

Through the passage we know as "the Great Commission," Jesus was clear about the Church's responsibility in global evangelism and disciple-making. However, Barna's study shows that the vocabulary and strategies surrounding the U.S. Church's commitment to this mandate are perhaps less clear. Misconceptions about missions and even concerns about its potential for misuse are not uncommon among churchgoers. Meanwhile, U.S. pastors continue to work toward their own definitions and conclusions about the best way to "go into all the world"—and their insight is sorely needed.

Pastors have an opportunity to inform the way churchgoers see, describe and participate in the Great Commission. Drawing from what Barna has observed in this study, this should happen . . .

> Pastors have an opportunity to inform the way churchgoers see, describe and participate in the Great Commission

PUBLICLY AND FREQUENTLY

One in four churchgoers who is involved in missions credits that decision to a direct invitation from their church. Church leaders remind Christians of their calling to proclaim and live out the gospel, as well as expose them to opportunities to do so. This task can't be limited only to the occasional announcement, newsletter or "special service."

How often do your weekly sermons mention the subject of missions? Does your church partner with organizations or missionaries—and, if so, do you educate your congregants on the details and impact of those relationships? Are members given many chances to learn, donate or even travel in support of those efforts? Do you provide updates or times of corporate prayer for missionaries and missions partners?

WITH PRECISION AND FEELING

Not only do a lot of U.S. churchgoers remain unfamiliar with the language of "the Great Commission," they are also in the midst of a dizzying and at times heated deliberation about the place of evangelism and social justice. Thus, pastors today must choose their words about missions with great intention—perhaps even defining them as they do so.

Further, a connection to a cause happens on a heart level, through what is said as well as what is felt. Churchgoers tell Barna they've previously been stirred to act because of a sense of purpose or because they heard a moving story about an area of need.

When leaders are both *precise* and *personal* in their messages about missions, they can help clarify the broader Church's calling to evangelism and justice, as well as mobilize their own congregants to be a part of it on a local and global level.

ALONGSIDE GOD'S WORD

This report points out that Bible-minded churchgoers in the U.S. show a deep understanding of and involvement in the Great Commission. Further, churchgoers and pastors feel that the Bible is important for life transformation, personal spiritual development and the success of missions. A strong theology of Christ-centered missions—addressing the needs of both the spiritual and physical person—appears to be just one byproduct of consistent and reverent study of scripture.

In a time when we see signs of skepticism toward evangelism and the Bible within the general population, and even within the Church itself, it might be tempting to treat scripture as secondary in missions and discipleship. But the Bible remains central in the revelation of God's love and the foundation of the Christian life. As David Daniels encourages (see his full Q&A on page 67), "[Pastors] help their people see the logical connection of a text to their personal lives. They unpack the complexities of scripture to reveal a book that is a divine masterpiece instead of an ordinary, human work. They train, counsel, marry and bury on the foundation of God's Word so that their people learn that scripture is food for life."

As your ministry continues to equip people for regular and rich study of the Bible, consider how your global missions involvement also emphasizes the gospel, making it accessible, relatable and transformative to as many people as possible.

5 SHIFTS RESHAPING MISSIONS

by Mark Matlock and David Kinnaman

It could be argued that not since the Reformation have we lived in a time when every aspect of life has been disrupted by sweeping changes, primarily brought on by the internet and globalization. Missions has experienced these disruptions as well, and they have some positive effects, if we will lean into them. Previous barriers have all but disappeared as advances in communication and travel have created incredible opportunities for the spreading of the gospel in our world.

This study presents many implications for the Church today as it relates to the sharing of Jesus' Good News. While the research shows definitions and ideas of missions are all over the map, much of this is the result of how we as a Church are coming to internalize and embrace several external developments in the field.

Here are five shifts we see occurring and believe all Christians should be mindful of in experiencing the Great Commission:

1. FROM PARACHURCH TO LOCAL CHURCH

While many missions breakthroughs in the 20th century occurred outside traditional church settings, the need for parachurch organizations is decreasing as churches build smarter and stronger collaborations that extend beyond financial capital. Previously, there have been certain kinds of expertise that parachurches alone could provide. Now, churches are empowered by local capability, information access, instant communication, travel and more. While the need for parachurch ministry still exists, especially in technical missions such as Bible translation, it's a more shared endeavor, working with local expressions of the church as well as other impact partners and organizations.

MARK MATLOCK
President of WisdomWorks

Mark has been serving the church and Bible translation community for more than two decades. He is the president of WisdomWorks, former executive director for Youth Specialties and creator of the PlanetWisdom student conferences. Currently he is helping unite churches to see scripture translated into the remaining languages within a decade through the Imagine Zero campaign. He has written several books for teens and parents and he is co-authoring the forthcoming book *Faith for Exiles* with David Kinnaman. Mark has also served on the board of directors of Seed Company and is currently on the board of the American Bible Society. He and his family live in Texas and attend Irving Bible Church, where he was ordained and serves as a teaching pastor.

2. FROM SENDING TO COLLABORATING

The Western Church still gravitates toward a sending model, and this is reinforced by our short-term missions approach. While the need to send missionaries remains, it is evolving as a result of globalized Christianity. Meanwhile, *mutual* assistance and support among partners around the world leverages opportunities for missions work to make greater impact.

3. FROM WESTERN CHURCH TO MAJORITY WORLD CHURCH

It's difficult for most churches in the U.S. to grasp the strength of non-Western churches today, which now comprise the majority of Christians in the world. Perhaps the greatest value of Americans participating in short-term trips is a raised awareness of the truly global Church—being able to witness and experience what God is doing elsewhere, rather than believing "we" are the originators of the gospel message.

4. FROM OUTPUTS TO IMPACT

Western missions has focused mostly on *counting outcomes*, such as the number of churches started, Bibles translated or disciples made. Today, missions is also concerned with *assessing the life transformation* resulting from those outcomes. This means starting with holistic strategies aided by the lenses of social science and research, and concluding by documenting and reporting positive impacts of missions efforts. For instance, Bible translation today isn't just about completing a translation; it's an integrated effort to see that work used as quickly as possible.

5. FROM "BREATHING OUT" TO "BREATHING IN"

Lessons learned from past colonial approaches to missions, along with the rise of the Church in the majority world, require mutual learning rather than one-way teaching. In other words, Christian workers don't just "go into all the world" to share; they go to learn as well. This humility is strengthening the global Church movement.

DAVID KINNAMAN
President of Barna Group

David is the author of the bestselling books *Good Faith*, *You Lost Me* and *unChristian*. He is president of the Barna Group, a leading research and communications company that works with churches, nonprofits and business ranging from film studios to financial services. Since 1995, David has directed interviews with nearly one million individuals and overseen hundreds of U.S. and global research studies. He and Mark Matlock are co-authors of the forthcoming book *Faith for Exiles*. He lives in California with his wife and their three children.

Every era of the Church lives during challenging and exciting times, and this is absolutely true as we continue into the 21st Century and new paradigms emerge. For the sake of people waiting for the gospel message—both now and in the future—we must do our part in the time and place to which God has called us.

> Christian workers don't just "go into all the world" to share; they go to learn as well

But you will receive power when
the Holy Spirit comes upon you.
And you will be my witnesses,
telling people about me everywhere—
in Jerusalem, throughout Judea, in Samaria,
and to the ends of the earth."

Acts 1:8 NLT

APPENDIX

A. NOTES

1. Robbie F. Castleman, "The Last Word: The Great Commission: Ecclesiology," *Themelios* 32, no. 3 (April 2007): 68–70, http://s3.amazonaws.com/tgc-documents/themelios/Themelios32.3.pdf.
2. Thomas Schirrmacher, "The Great Commission—An Exploration of the Old and New Testament," *Lausanne World Pulse*, July 2009, http://www.lausanneworldpulse.com/perspectives-php/1165/07-2009.
3. Center for the Study of Global Christianity, *Christianity in its Global Context, 1970–2020*, June 2013, http://www.gordonconwell.edu/resources/documents/1ChristianityinitsGlobalContext.pdf.
4. J. Herbert Kane, *The Making of a Missionary*, (Ada, MI: Baker Book House, 1975) 13.
5. Oxford Dictionaries, s.v. "social justice warrior," accessed January 25, 2018, https://en.oxforddictionaries.com/definition/us/social_justice_warrior.
6. Barna Group, *The Good News About Global Poverty*, (Ventura, CA: Barna Group, forthcoming).
7. "Andrew Walls: An Exiting Period in Christian History," *Faith & Leadership*, June 5, 2011, https://www.faithandleadership.com/andrew-walls-exciting-period-christian-history.
8. Barna Group, "Americans Soften on Immigration in 2017," September 19, 2017, https://www.barna.com/research/americans-soften-immigration-2017/.
9. Center for the Study of Global Christianity, *Christianity in its Global Context, 1970–2020*.
10. Andrew F. Walls, *The Missionary Movement in Christian History* (Maryknoll, NY: Orbis Books, 1996) 226.
11. "The History of the English Bible," Bible Odyssey, accessed January 25, 2018, https://www.bibleodyssey.org/en/tools/timeline-gallery/h/history-of-the-english-bible.
12. "The History of the English Bible," Bible Odyssey.
13. "History of English," English Club, accessed January 25, 2018, https://www.englishclub.com/history-of-english/.
14. George M. Cowan, "Bible Translation Since John Wycliffe," *Christian History*, Issue 3, 1983, https://christianhistoryinstitute.org/magazine/issue/john-wycliffe-bible-translator.
15. *Encyclopaedia Brittanica Online*, s.v. "William Carey," accessed January 25, 2018, https://www.britannica.com/biography/William-Carey.
16. Harriet Hill, "The Vernacular Treasure: A Century of Mother-Tongue Bible Translation," *International Bulletin of Missionary Research* 30, no. 2 (April 2006): 82–87, http://www.wycliffe.net/missiology?id=1210.
17. "William Cameron 'Uncle Cam' Townsend," The Encyclopedia of Arkansas History & Culture, accessed January 25, 2018, http://www.encyclopediaofarkansas.net/encyclopedia/entry-detail.aspx?entryID=4453.
18. Joan Huyser-Honig, "Ethnodoxology: Calling All Peoples to Worship in Their Heart Language," Calvin Institute of Christian Worship, February 10, 2009, https://worship.calvin.edu/resources/resource-library/ethnodoxology-calling-all-peoples-to-worship-in-their-heart-language/.
19. Wycliffe Bible Translators, "Empowering Families for Lasting Change," January 7, 2015, https://www.youtube.com/watch?v=tEJuV5VyER0.
20. Wycliffe Global Alliance, "2017 Bible Translation FAQ: Going Deeper," November 2017, http://resources.wycliffe.net/statistics/Wycliffe%20Global%20Alliance%20Statistics%202017%20FAQs_EN.pdf.
21. Harriet Hill, "The Vernacular Treasure."
22. Wycliffe Global Alliance, "2017 Bible Translation FAQ."
23. Harriet Hill, "The Vernacular Treasure."
24. Kwame Bediako, "The Role and Significance of the Translation of the Bible into African Languages in the Consolidation of the Church and Its Expansion into Unreached Areas," (Paper presented at Wycliffe Bible Translators International Africa Area Forum, Limuru, Kenya, May 16–18, 2001), http://www.wycliffe.net/missiology?id=1105.
25. "What Does the Term "Gospel" Mean?" Bible.org, accessed January 25, 2018, https://bible.org/question/what-does-term-%E2%80%9Cgospel%E2%80%9D-mean.

B. GLOSSARY

FAITH SEGMENTS

Practicing Christians are self-identified Christians who say their faith is very important in their lives and have attended a worship service within the past month.

Evangelicals meet nine criteria, which include having made a personal commitment to Jesus Christ that is still important in their life today and believing that, when they die, they will go to heaven because they have confessed their sins and accepted Jesus Christ as their Savior. The seven other conditions include saying their faith is very important in their lives; believing they have a personal responsibility to share their religious beliefs about Christ with non-Christians; believing that Satan exists; believing that Jesus Christ lived a sinless life on earth; asserting that the Bible is accurate in all that it teaches; believing that eternal salvation is possible only through grace, not works; and describing God as the all-knowing, all-powerful, perfect deity who created the universe and still rules it today. Being classified as an evangelical is not dependent on church attendance or denominational affiliation, and respondents are not asked to describe themselves as "evangelical."

GENERATION

Gen Z were born between 1999 and 2015.
Millennials were born between 1984 and 2002.
Gen X were born between 1965 and 1983.
Boomers were born between 1946 and 1964.
Elders were born prior to 1946.

DENOMINATION

Respondents were asked to identify the denomination or affiliation of the church they attend most often.

- *Mainline*: includes American Baptist Churches, Episcopal, Evangelical Lutheran Church of America, United Church of Christ, United Methodist, and Presbyterian Church, USA
- *Non-mainline*: includes Protestant churches not included in mainline denominations
- *Catholic*: includes those who describe themselves as Catholic

ETHNICITY

Ethnicity is based on respondents' self-descriptions of their ethnicity. Those who describe themselves as Hispanic plus another ethnicity are coded as Hispanic only. To ensure adequate sample sizes, Barna usually segments the population only by the three largest ethnic groups.

- White / Caucasian
- Black / African American
- Hispanic / Latino
- Asian
- Other / more than one race and not defined in any of the above

C. THE IMPACT OF BIBLE AWARENESS

Given the scope of the topics covered in this study, the analysts were curious if more biblically minded or knowledgeable individuals might have unique reactions to the questions. For example, does knowing that the Bible is not originally an American or a European text make U.S. adults more interested in ensuring Bible translation for other people groups? Does familiarity with Jesus' life influence ideas about completing the mission he left to his followers?

Barna came up with a simple scoring system based on two series of questions, about the life of Jesus Christ and about the context in which the gospel message is communicated. The researchers then created custom groups that reveal how different levels of awareness of these aspects manifest in the data. This report highlights these knowledge differences among churchgoers in order to give insight into the variety of ways of thinking about and communicating the Great Commission.

KNOWLEDGE OF GOSPEL CONTEXT

Barna asked respondents four questions that pertain to an awareness of the origins and languages of scripture: how many languages exist in the world, how many languages have a Bible translation, which languages were originally used to write the Bible and what is the original definition of "gospel."

The term "gospel," which stems from the Old English term *Godspell*, meaning "good tale," has come to mean a range of things in modern English—depending on your denomination (or even just your editorial style guide!). But there is a direct translation from

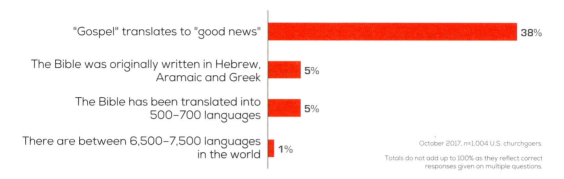

the Greek word *euangelion* (where we also get the term "evangelism")—meaning "good news"[25]—and more than a third of churchgoers (38%) recognize this interpretation.

In surveying about knowledge of scriptural context, respondents were also presented with a list of 11 languages and asked to identify the ones in which the Bible was originally written. Just one in 20 churchgoers (5%) correctly selects versions of Hebrew, Aramaic and Greek. Barna did give partial credit for this knowledge score to churchgoers who chose *any* of the three correct languages.

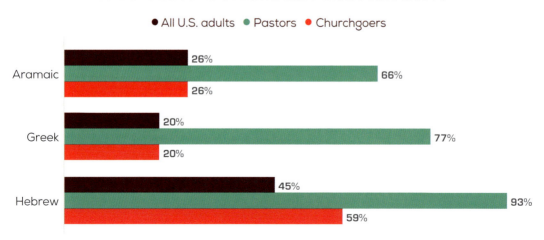

Overall, churchgoers lack some details about how many languages have a Bible translation, as well as how many global languages there are in the first place. Just 1 percent correctly note a range of 6,500 to 7,500 languages in the world, and 5 percent rightly assume that between 500 and 700 languages have completed Bible translations. Incorrect responses about global languages and scriptural translations drive down the overall scores for knowledge of the context of the gospel.

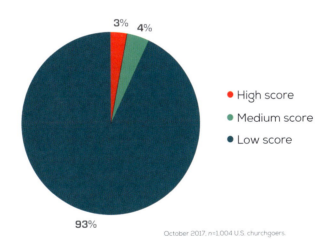

- High level of knowledge = correctly answer 2.5–3 out of 4 questions (partial credit is given for correctly identifying at least one language of the Bible)
- Medium level of knowledge = correctly answer 2 out of 4 questions
- Low level of knowledge = correctly answer 0 or 1 out of 4 questions

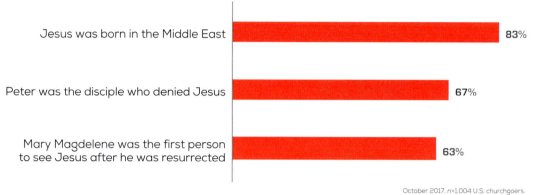

KNOWLEDGE OF THE NEW TESTAMENT

Barna asked respondents a set of three questions about some key details from the life of Jesus, as communicated in the New Testament, including: Jesus' birthplace, the name of the disciple who denied Christ and the name of the follower who first saw Jesus after the resurrection. Responses show that the majority of the general population and churchgoing Americans is informed about some prominent details from the Gospels.

The level of knowledge of Jesus' life does make a difference in how a churchgoer thinks about a broad range of topics: missions and its relationship to social justice, meeting spiritual and physical needs, the role of Bible translation in missions and the significance of scripture in spiritual development. These scores also correspond to churchgoers' faith practice: Three-quarters of those with a high score (77%) have been to church in the past week, compared with about six in 10 of the groups with lower scores (62% of medium or low scores).

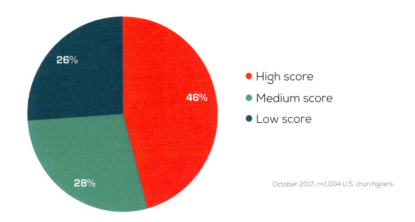

- High level of knowledge = correctly answer all questions
- Medium level of knowledge = correctly answer 2 out of the 3 questions
- Low level of knowledge = correctly answer 1 or 0 out of the 3 questions

BIBLE MINDEDNESS

Barna first defined and developed the "Bible minded" group in research conducted with American Bible Society and has been tracking it for roughly seven years. It's a way of measuring those who regularly engage with the Bible and believe it is relevant to their lives. Bible-minded churchgoers report reading the Bible in the past week and strongly assert the Bible is accurate in the principles it teaches.

Other categories show less engagement with and sometimes less trust of the Bible. These categories are the aggregate of respondents' reading habits and beliefs about the Bible.

- Bible minded: read the Bible within the past seven days *and* agree strongly that the Bible is accurate
- Bible disciplined: read the Bible within the past seven days *but* do not agree strongly that the Bible is accurate
- Bible dormant: have not read the Bible within the past seven days *but* agree strongly or somewhat that the Bible is accurate
- Bible skeptic: have not read the Bible within the past seven days *and* disagree strongly or somewhat that the Bible is accurate

Unsurprisingly, churchgoers are more likely to be Bible minded when they know more about the Bible and about its language context in the series of knowledge questions. More than half of those with a high level of knowledge of the New Testament (54%) are also Bible minded. One in four of those with low knowledge of gospel context (23%) is Bible minded.

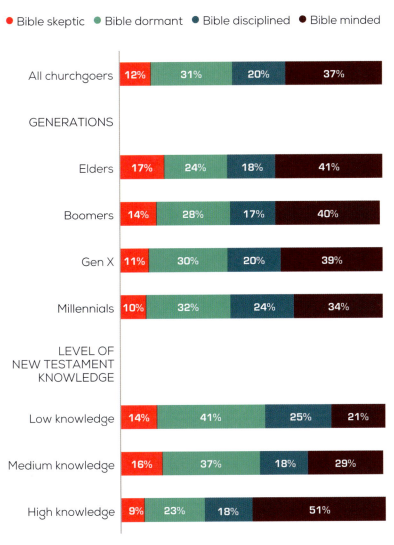

THE IMPACT OF BIBLE AWARENESS

D. METHODOLOGY

This study involved qualitative and quantitative research with pastors, churchgoers and U.S. adults.

In initial research, an open-ended online survey was conducted in July 2017 to explore perceptions of missions and Bible translation. The 84 participants included 25 pastors, 31 practicing Christians (of any age) and 28 churchgoing Millennials.

Subsequently, Barna surveyed the same types of respondents in a comprehensive online survey made up of primarily closed-end quantitative questions. These interviews were conducted in October 2017 with a nationally representative sample of 1,010 U.S. adults, as well as 619 U.S. Protestant senior pastors (senior, lead or executive roles) and 1,004 U.S. adult churchgoers (who have attended a regular church service within the past six months). An oversample of young adults contributed to a total of 692 Millennial churchgoing respondents.

E. ACKNOWLEDGMENTS

Barna Group is grateful to Seed Company for their partnership in *Translating the Great Commission* and their commitment to making the Bible available to every person. We're especially appreciative of Mark Matlock for championing this study.

A thank you to the following Seed Company members for their contributions and review of the survey and report: Michael Currier, Gilles Gravelle, Doug Kogler, Davis Powell, Nathan Rittenhouse, Jaki Rix, Kraig Thompson and Mike Toupin.

A special thanks to the contributors who completed these pages with their insights and expertise: Allen Yeh, David Daniels and Joyce Williams.

The research for this project was led by Brooke Hempell and Traci Hochmuth. Under the editorial direction of Roxanne Stone, Susan Mettes provided analysis of the data and Alyce Youngblood compiled and edited this report. Doug Brown proofed the manuscript. Annette Allen created the cover and data visualizations, and Rob Williams designed the layout and interior pages. Brenda Usery managed production with help from Todd White. Our supportive Barna colleagues include Amy Brands, Bill Denzel, David Kinnaman, Steve McBeth, Elise Miller, Anna Reese, Caitlin Schuman and Jess Villa.

F. ABOUT THE PROJECT PARTNERS

Barna Group is a research firm dedicated to providing actionable insights on faith and culture, with a particular focus on the Christian church. Since 1984, Barna has conducted more than one million interviews in the course of hundreds of studies, and has become a go-to source for organizations that want to better understand a complex and changing world from a faith perspective.

Barna's clients and partners include a broad range of academic institutions, churches, nonprofits and businesses, such as Alpha, Compassion International, the Templeton Foundation, Fuller Seminary, the Bill and Melinda Gates Foundation, Maclellan Foundation, DreamWorks Animation, Focus Features, Habitat for Humanity, The Navigators, NBC-Universal, the ONE Campaign, Paramount Pictures, the Salvation Army, Walden Media, Sony and World Vision. The firm's studies are frequently quoted by major media outlets such as *The Economist*, BBC, CNN, *USA Today*, the *Wall Street Journal*, Fox News, Huffington Post, *The New York Times* and the *Los Angeles Times*.

www.Barna.com

Seed Company is an organization that helps link donors to locally driven Bible translation projects, with a mission to provide scripture to all languages by the year 2025. Since launching in 1993, Seed has helped contribute to Bible translations in 1,000 languages, spanning 90 countries and 6 continents, with the help of 24,000 prayer and financial partners. It is a subsidiary organization of Wycliffe USA and a participant in the Wycliffe Global Alliance. .

www.TheSeedCompany.org

Stay Informed About Cultural Trends

Barna Trends 2018
A beautifully designed and engaging look at today's trending topics that includes new data, analysis, infographics, and interviews right at your fingertips.

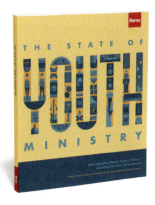

State of Youth Ministry
A wide-angle view of the youth ministry landscape that will spark conversations and lead to more effective student ministries, healthier youth workers, and sturdier teen faith.

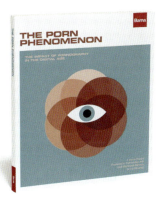

The Porn Phenomenon
This study exposes the breadth and depth of pornography's impact and confirms that we can no longer ignore its impact on the next generation.

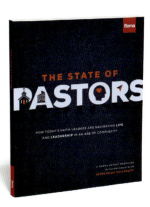

The State of Pastors
Pastoring in a complex cultural moment is not easy. Read about how church leaders are holding up in this whole-life assessment of U.S. pastors.

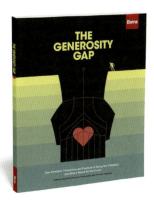

The Generosity Gap
Generosity is changing. Read about how pastors and laypeople perceive and practice generosity, and learn methods for strengthening giving habits.

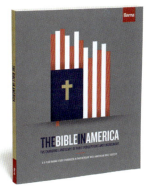

The Bible in America
Analysis, insights and encouragement for those who want to understand Scripture engagement today and how to cultivate faith that lasts in an ever-changing world.

AVAILABLE AT BARNA.COM/RESOURCES

Meet the Next, Next Generation

The research explores the following:

- Statistics on teens' views of themselves, their spiritual lives, and the world
- Comparative data with older generations of adults
- Barna analysis of cultural trends driving Gen Z
- Infographics and data visualizations

National ministries, local churches, and Barna Group have been talking for years about generational differences, especially when it comes to young adults born between 1984 and 2002: the Millennials. But now a new generation is becoming a cultural force in their own right. *Gen Z: The Culture, Beliefs, and Motivations Shaping the Next Generation* is Barna's first major research study investigating the perceptions, experiences, and motivations of teens in Generation Z. In partnership with Impact 360, the study is our best thinking thus far on the values, assumptions, and allegiances of teens in the next, next generation. This definitive report is a must-read for pastors and parents as they help tomorrow's Christian leaders grow.

Learn more at
whoisgenz.com

Society Is Changing—How Should Christians Respond?

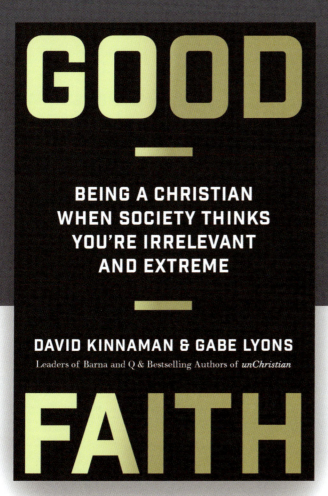

You will learn

- How to respond with compassion and confidence to the most challenging issues of our day
- The cultural trends that are creating both obstacles and opportunities for Christians
- The heart behind opposing views and how to stay friends despite differences.
- How to empower a new generation to hold to their beliefs while loving their friends

Society is changing its mind about the Christian way of thinking and living. *Good Faith* includes vast amounts of new research documenting the increasing cultural tensions and fault lines between faithful Christians and the wider public. Christians are increasingly viewed as irrelevant and extremist and must figure out how to respond.

Good Faith is for everyone—from students to retirees, parents to grandparents, and Millennials to Boomers—who wants to be informed and equipped to live as a Christian in a complex, changing culture. You will come away with new ideas and inspiration to live and lead with love that is grounded in belief.

Purchase wherever books and ebooks are sold

Learn more at barna.com/goodfaith